Group Counseling and Psychotherapy with Adolescents

Beryce W. MacLennan
and Naomi Felsenfeld

Columbia University Press
New York and London

Beryce W. MacLennan is a Clinical and Community Psychologist and serves as Chief of Consultation and Community Liaison at the Mental Health Study Center, National Institute of Mental Health.

Naomi Felsenfeld is Core supervisor at the New Careers Training Program, Georgetown University-Freeman, Cole and Associates, Washington, D. C.

This work was supported in part by Grant No. 64221, Office of Juvenile Delinquency and Youth Development, U. S. Department of Health, Education and Welfare.

Copyright © 1968 Columbia University Press
International Standard Book Number 0-231-08640-7
Third printing and Columbia Paperback Edition 1970
Printed in the United States of America

Preface

This book has been written to serve as an aid in the development and conceptualization of group programs for adolescents in all kinds of settings and as a basic text for those interested in learning group methods. We have particularly sought to identify the commonalities in all levels of group management concerned with individual adjustment and change and have attempted to present the material so that it can be useful to professionals and subprofessionals who are working with either normal or emotionally disturbed youth.

We believe that the boundaries between the normal and the abnormal are fluid and a matter of judgment, that all people go through periods of trouble and increased stress from time to time, and that problems are normal. What matters is how the individual copes with problems and how the social system reacts. Our experiences in developing Human Service Aide Training programs and in consulting with many agencies have made us become increasingly clear in our own minds that problems are most frequently exasperated and magnified because of the system's refusal to acknowledge and deal with its own disfunction and that it is usually inappropriate to create special settings for the management of particular problems because this stigmatizes the individual and supports scapegoating and evasion by the social system. Thus, we emphasize wherever possible the use of group intervention in normal settings.

We have become convinced, too, that it is essential to understand the larger society, the culture, the institutional structure and functioning, the development and peer-group pressures to which the individual is subject as well as his particular personality and situation in order to help him work out his problems and increase his life satisfaction. Therefore, we have included a basic consideration of the organization of society and chapters on general group theory and the adolescent and his culture as well as on our particular approaches to group counseling and group psychotherapy. In our chapter on the group leader and his training, we have stressed the importance of the leader's management of himself and our conviction that, provided he is a sensitive person capable of self-understanding, perceptiveness, and concern for others, a leader does not require a higher education for many types of group management but can be trained relatively quickly to counsel effectively.

These ideas have evolved out of years of experience with youngsters in all kinds of groups in many different programs. It is impossible to acknowledge all the boys and girls, colleagues, teachers, and agency staffs who have contributed to this learning; but a few stand out. For MacLennan, the most significant early influences were Edward Shils, who first aroused her interest in groups; S. R. Slavson, who taught her group therapy and how to work with adolescents; for Felsenfeld, her first supervisor, George Brager, and her experiences at the Mt. Vernon YM and YWHA.

Both feel indebted to William Klein, Arthur Pearl, and J. Douglas Grant, who helped us to clarify thinking and to conceptualize and evaluate our programs. We should particularly like to thank Seymour Rosenthal for his staunch support and our secretaries, Sibyl Pusti and Naomi Levy, for the long hours they have spent and the invaluable assistance they have given us in the preparation of the book, and to Mrs. Levy for her preparation of an excellent index. Our acknowledgments are also accorded to the Center for Youth and Community Studies, Howard University, and the Office of Juvenile Delinquency and Youth Crime under whose auspices the original manuscript was written.

Beryce W. MacLennan, Ph. D.
Naomi Felsenfeld, ACSW

Contents

I

Introduction

...hildren and youth to behave in ... vital part of its self-perpetua... is of socialization. When children ... the socially expected fashion, ..., or inadequately trained; and retraining procedures become necessary. This is the process of rehabilitation.

Thus, the goals of socialization and rehabilitation are essentially similar. Both are concerned that the individual learn to live a full and satisfying life in the context of the society within which he finds himself.

However, for youth in Western society the processes of socialization and rehabilitation have been separated. We have called the first education, training, normal development; the second, treatment, therapy, rehabilitation, the correction of pathology and delinquency. We have developed separate institutions. For the first, we have the family, the school, the church, recreation, cultural and special interest groups; for the second —which is essentially concerned with the failures of the first— we have guidance clinics, casework agencies, court services, mental and correctional institutions, and welfare agencies.

What have been the consequences of this? In the first place, it has led to a diversion of many of the most knowledgeable and highly trained people in human dynamics and interrelationships from the normal institutions into those concerned with pathology. It has led to a de-emphasizing of the socialization process within normal institutions and to a focusing on content and the assimilation of knowledge, skill, and technique rather than on the development of sound human relationships; and it has relieved these institutions from the responsibility for the failures of their training procedures.

It has reinforced what appears to be a normal tendency for a group which contains an element within itself too different, deviant, or difficult to deal with, to polarize it, to extrude it, or to drive it out. We see this daily with the youth who is disturbing in the classroom, makes trouble on the street, is too disruptive in therapy or training groups, or is unmanageable in an institution to which he has been confined for delinquency or pathological deviancy. This polarization and extrusion provide a mechanism whereby society is able to avoid examining how the institutions which are concerned with normal socialization or even rehabilitation are functioning.

This has meant that large segments of society are conceived of as unacceptable and excluded from an opportunity to lead satisfying lives. It has meant that the institutions concerned with normal development are unable to deal with the many people who have inappropriate standards and unrealistic expectations and who are consequently dissatisfied with their lives. It has meant that many people who are floundering, but who are unwilling to stigmatize themselves as pathological, crazy, or delinquent, are unable to ask for help. It has meant that those institutions concerned with pathology are cut off from the normal community resources which they require in order to assist people to remake their lives.

These considerations raise many questions about the organization of society, community mental health, and the training and allocation of human service personnel.

For example, are child guidance clinics and community psychiatric clinics, juvenile courts and correctional institutions really functional? How can we change our normal institutions so they are really concerned with the training of our children to lead satisfying lives? How can we reorganize and coordinate and make relevant our resources so that they can be applied with maximal effectiveness? What do people need to know in order to become effective parents and teachers and recreational group workers? Should not many more of our psychiatrists, psychologists, and sociologists be trained as consultants to the normal institutions? What kinds of normal counseling for life, such as training for marriage and parenthood, should these normal institutions provide?

All these different institutions are concerned with the training or retraining of youth, and in all their activities there are components which deal with the development of satisfactory human relationships. Improved functioning consequently can be achieved not only through changes in the individual but also through the reorganization of the structure and functioning of institutions and change in the values and the norms of the society in which the individual lives. There are essentially several approaches to achieving individual and social change: (1) working with the individual alone or with others to change himself and to acquire skills and knowledge; (2) creating new group pressures which impinge on the individual and move him to change; (3) creating and changing community structures, institutions, or neighborhoods which can provide opportunities for the individual to live a satisfying life. This book will concentrate on methods of working with adolescents in small groups for the purpose of helping them solve their normal developmental problems (group counseling) or to reassess themselves and to react differently to problems and situations which have led them into trouble and unhappiness (psychotherapy). Frequently, it is hard to distinguish counseling and therapy; and sometimes it is preferable to treat them both as essential parts of other activities, such as recreation, learning, or working at a job.

Both group counseling and group psychotherapy involve change for the individuals who are members of the group and the creation of a group climate which will in turn affect the individual. Thus, in order to be able to control such groups of adolescents, it is necessary to understand that particular phase of the growth continuum. It is also necessary to be familiar with the community and culture from which group members are drawn and to understand the relationship between the group and the setting within which it is taking place. One should be able to understand the individual members, their behavior, their feelings, and their needs. Further, it is essential to perceive what is going on in the group and how the members are interacting and affecting each other. Whenever one tries to help individuals modify their behavior, it is useful to have some idea of the processes through which change can be achieved. Finally, it is always necessary to understand one's own reaction to the group as a whole and to the individuals within it.

In training people to undertake group counseling or group psychotherapy, it is necessary to make concepts meaningful; relate theory to practice; increase the individual's capacity to perceive and comprehend group and individual behavior and to manage himself so that he reacts appropriately and with correct timing.

No interventions should be undertaken without clear program conceptualization, program control, and evaluation. At the start, it is essential to establish a baseline. What is the population like? Who will undertake the intervention and under what conditions? What is it planned to change? What does the leader plan to do? What kind of interaction does he anticipate? What results does he hope for? How will he determine whether he has been successful? Then, even if only in the simplest way, the leader should check whether the program goes according to plan and whether the interactions are as expected. Finally, outcomes should be examined and the program refined in terms of the results.

In the next chapter, group properties which are relevant to group management will be discussed and some methods of group study described. Then, before moving into an examination of methods of group counseling and group psychotherapy, the dimensions of Western culture and the special tasks of adolescents will be considered.

II

The Group as an Agent of Change

Groups as Change Agents

In this book, groups are examined as vehicles for helping the individual change his self concepts, his self management, and his way of life. Group conditions are established for several purposes:

1. To provide constructive experience which will assist the individual to feel differently about himself and others;
2. To give support or to add pressure to the individual's attempt to behave differently;
3. To provide opportunities for the individual to discuss and examine problems which he experiences in all areas of his life;
4. To give the individual a chance to examine and analyze his impact on others as it is expressed in the group itself.

In order to create such conditions, it is necessary to understand what groups are, how they develop, and how they function. It is also important to explore the conditions under which change can take place. Emphasis here is primarily on those aspects of small face-to-face groups which seem most relevant for counseling and psychotherapy. Some consideration will be given to the dynamics of institutions and communities.

The Development of a Group

A group is a dynamic entity. It does not start fully developed but must in time create its identity, decide on its direction, its ways of operating, and become a small social system in its own right. It is composed of a number of people who come together for some common purpose. In order to function, members must communicate and interact; thus, size is important. They must be identifiable to each other, become acquainted, define the purposes of the group implicitly or explicitly. They must develop a way of interacting, establish rules and limits, formally or informally. The group, to endure, must be able to hold its members. It must satisfy their needs, have attraction for them. This is called group cohesion. The members become interdependent. They become aware of each other, have meaning and concern for each other. If a member is missing or leaves the group or if someone new joins, the group is no longer the same. The group becomes a part of each member's life. It becomes one of his reference groups, and he has a sense of belonging to the group. When a group ends, this means a change in the lives of all its members. Members may initially come to the group under pressure; but if the group is to form and become a viable entity, members must come to feel this sense of belonging and to accept their part in the group and some responsibility for it. Thus, consent is ultimately crucial. Members come for some common purpose; but they also have their separate needs, their hidden agendas, and there will be struggles to reconcile these in the group and pressure for members to conform to the demands of the group as a whole and to reach agreement. Members also try to know how they stand in relation to each other in the group. They adopt certain roles. Some kind of status hierarchy will develop which is a focus of conflict and is unlikely to remain static. Thus, there is always struggle and tension within the group, dynamic interaction; and the climate of the group will depend on these struggles and the way they are carried on. There are also contrary movements in the group for it to change or to remain the same. At any time the forces within the group may be in flux or temporarily in equilibrium.

For groups to start or continue, some member or members must take the initiative, show leadership; and struggles may center in the group on who will have the most influence and power. Groups vary in how they operate, in the kind of leadership, the degree of participation of members, the amount of tension and conflict, the kind of climate which is customary when they meet, and the degree to which they demand conformity from the members or the extent to which they can tolerate deviance, disequilibrium, and ambiguity. Groups do not function in a vacuum but within a physical setting and a larger organizational structure; within an institution or an open community. The quality of the setting and the relationship of the group to the larger organization affects its functioning and imposes limitations on it.

Differences between a group and a crowd are numerous. A crowd is anonymous, there is no clear sense of interdependence, members do not know each other. They can come and go without appreciably affecting the whole. The ground rules for a crowd are established impersonally by the circumstances. A crowd can easily become a mob because there is no sense of personal responsibility to the whole. In a mob, and sometimes in a crowd, there is a surrender of personal direction, judgment, and responsibility for decision-making. Members cease to think decisively. They follow chance leadership, can be caught up easily in emotional currents. Emotional contagion, described by Redl,[1] where members respond to others by adopting the same emotional expression, is a phenomenon in all groups, but is more likely to occur and is more extensive in crowds than in small groups. This is an aspect of the concept of deindividualization in which individuals surrender their autonomy and emotional control.

[1] Redl, "Group Emotion and Leadership," *Psychiatry,* V (1942), 573–96.

The Beginning of a Group

Groups may form spontaneously through people finding themselves together in a similar situation, such as holiday-makers in a resort or children on a street; or someone may take the initiative in calling people together.

A new group is an ambiguous situation, and the members strive to reduce this ambiguity. They want to find out what the group is about, what it will do, what the purposes of the group are, how it will operate, what the other members are like, how they will relate to each other. They try to develop structure.

In the beginning, members deal with superficialities. They inquire about names and affiliations. They examine each other and make beginning judgments about them. They try and assess whether it will be a pleasant or painful experience. People who are strangers to each other feel in a dangerous position. They do not know what the others are like, how powerful they are, how much they can hurt them, and consequently are reluctant to expose themselves and to trust each other. Involvement should increase with time.

Names

People have primitive feelings about names, for one's name is part of one's identity. When one's name is known, one can be traced and held responsible for one's acts so that power is given to others. Names and titles give information about a member's position in the world. Names have particular associations. They remind one of other people in one's past experience, and one often attributes characteristics and has expectations from people with particular names. They are expected to act in certain ways and fulfill certain roles.

Physical Assessment

When members first meet, they often seem to have little individuality. Although some stand out, others are hard to identify. People are judged initially by physical appearance and outward characteristics: how they dress, their expressions, muscular tension, movements and gestures, grooming, tone of voice, and what they say. Again, judgments are made on the basis of past experience. Just as with names, members expect people who resemble others in their past lives to behave in similar ways, and members react to them as if they were similar. These expectations are the basis of transference, that is, relating to a person in the present in terms of past relationship with significant people in one's life, so that one attributes qualities and reacts in ways which may not be appropriate to present reality.

Cliques

As members become acquainted, cliques and alliances form. In a dynamic group, these will not become set but will change, forming and reforming in accordance with the needs of the members at any particular time. Formal structure with the development of positions and ranks tends to interfere with this fluid and dynamic interaction.

Individual Defenses Against Anxiety

Individuals react to insecurity, anxiety, and to becoming part of a group in different ways. Some individuals stay very quiet. They do not want to risk exposing themselves until they are sure of their ground. They may sit and say nothing, but they are very aware of what is going on. Other individuals who are silent may be so anxious that they are not even aware of what is going on.

They may go blank, may be overcome by and only aware of fear, or, when anxious, they may retreat into a world of their own and indulge in fantasy. Others who are silent may be expecting to be called upon. They manage uncertain situations by waiting to be told what to do. Some, when anxious, begin to expect that they will be pushed around and get set in a resistive position to give as little as possible. Still others who are silent feel powerful, knowing more about the rest than the other members know of them.

Many members attempt to deal actively with an anxious situation. Some members ask many questions. They try and get the leader to define the situation. They become good and eager pupils, or they place themselves in a superior position as the assistant to the leader and attempt to draw others out. Some members begin actively to assert themselves, to define the group in their terms and to struggle to gain mastery and overthrow the leader, or if there is no leader, to assume this position.

Other members handle their discomfort through expressions of dissatisfaction and complaint. Often members will attempt to obtain allies by searching out those with whom they can have something in common. Members may strive to know their position by comparing themselves with others and taking the initiative in obtaining information from others for this purpose. Members may also protect themselves by seeking out someone as the butt in the group and leading an attack on that member.

Group Defenses

The group as a whole deals with anxiety by attempting to reduce ambiguity. The members attempt to define their purposes and goals, understand what each wants, decide how they will operate, and find out how they stand in relation to each other. They look for someone to take responsibility for these interactions. If there is a designated leader, they expect him to take these responsibilities on; and if he does not, they are likely to become resentful. They are evincing a mechanism, "the dependency demand," identified by Bion [2] as a group defense and very commonly seen at the beginning of a group.

Bion, influenced on the one hand by Gestalt psychology—which was concerned with viewing the individual within the context of his total social and emotional situation—and on the other by Klein's psychoanalytic theory with its emphasis on the early months of an infant's life, distinguished between the group task, the overt content of the group, which he named the work group, and underlying dynamic interactions. He identified three principal defenses in groups at this second level, essentially ways in which the group resists change. He called these defenses basic assumptions and identified them as the "dependency demand," "flight and fight," and "pairing." A variety of group operations are included under these headings. In the "dependency demand" state, group members may evince helpless dependent behavior, complaining, asking for help, passive dependency. The dependency can be manifested in the group by members talking about their longing to have the leader to themselves, asking for individual interviews, talking about how they hated sharing when they were young. It is important to recognize that such demands may have no basis in reality. An individual who says he cannot talk about certain kinds of information in the group may not really be concerned with this at all. He may be primarily motivated by his desire to be taken care of and given in to by the leader.

Fighting can very clearly be seen as a way of avoiding getting down to business, although the real purpose is sometimes obscured by the sound and fury. A group may be unable to face conflict and difference and consequently whenever it reaches such a point may break up. A struggle around who shall give or who shall do the work can successfully get in the way of any change being accomplished.

2 Bion, *Experience in Groups.*

The third assumption—pairing—is often harder to identify. It occurs when the group sits back and allows two members to cooperate in diverting the group from its work. A clear example was seen in a group where a leader was asking the members whether they were satisfied with the group. Before anyone could talk, a supervisor, made anxious by this invitation to criticize, moved in and went into a long eulogy about the group, the leader, and how no one could be dissatisfied, making it very hard indeed for the leader to get to the cause of the difficulty. The supervisor successfully paired with the leader and cut him off from the group.

Particularly in the early stages of the group, members are very concerned about whether it will be a "good" group, a successful one, with status in the outside world. They become concerned that the other members will also think that the group is a "good" group.

Group Belonging

Members become affiliated and identify with the group. They belong and talk about "we," "us," and "ours." There is a process of partial de-individualization in which the members identify with the group. They make it a part of themselves and surrender part of their autonomy to the group in return for the satisfaction they gain from it. Thus, any slur on the group is also a reflection on them. If a member rejects the group and leaves, the others become anxious; will everyone leave? Will the group fall apart and cease to exist? If the group is no good, are they also no good? They feel they personally have failed to satisfy the needs of the departing member. There is anger at the leader for failing to do his part in keeping the member. Also, in any group centered around a leader, there is an element of the family; and members compete for the leader and the leader's attention and love. There are always mixed feelings about other members because this means sharing the leader. Sibling rivalry is always great; and there is both the desire to work together and gain each other's support and to kill each other off, so that when a member leaves, each member feels guilt that in some way he has participated in driving him out of the group.

Group Stages

Groups tend to go through different stages depending on their purposes and goals. Bales [3] and other social scientists have studied the process of problem-solving groups in terms of identifying the problem, problem breakdown and analysis, and problem reconstruction. In therapy groups, adolescents have been described as going through phases of initial politeness and good behavior; griping, testing, and acting out; dependency and demandingness; and ultimately mature problem-solving and separation to lead a more independent and self-reliant life.

Groups operate and can be studied at several different levels. On the surface, they will be concerned with the overt purpose of the group, whether it be having fun, helping each other solve problems, understanding themselves better, or performing some task. The group as a whole will be forming and changing, developing or reorganizing structure, adopting standards. Members will be relating to each other, competing, forming alliances, taking on roles, adapting themselves to the demands of the group.

Dynamic Interaction an Essential of Change

For the group to become an effective agent of change, dynamic tension must be maintained. When a group is in equilibrium, no change is taking place. It is only when there is conflict and the meeting of opposing views and actions that change can take place. When a group or an individual is in the process of change, no one knows the outcome; but inevitably the indi-

[3] Bales, *Interaction Process Analysis*.

vidual and the group will be different. Individuals will have to change their concepts of themselves and will have to give up certain beliefs or ways of behaving in favor of others. Consequently, in order for individuals to change they must feel admiration for others who represent the new. They must see advantages for themselves and the need to be able to be a part of something new and exciting. Thus, change always involves some insecurity, anxiety, and discomfort, although it may also bring many satisfactions. Conflict in some degree is essential for change.

Because of these anxieties about change, groups are more effective if they can not only develop enough consensus to put pressure on their members but can also provide enough support so that members can feel that it is not too dangerous to trust each other, to expose themselves, and to test reality in the group. A climate needs to be created in which members can respect each other and in which confrontation can be undertaken constructively. If change is desired, there are always mixed feelings; and change is achieved through working with this ambivalence in the group. Groups operate in terms of the values which are rewarded by the group so that groups concerned with individual change should emphasize the importance of facing reality, the importance of respecting oneself and others, the willingness to become involved with each other; to become intimate, to be frank, and to reveal the things which are of importance to one. If there is a leader, he should be willing to demonstrate these values in action.

Intimacy is always a two-way proposition. It implies closeness, knowledge, and acceptance between partners. It necessitates willingness to trust each other and to reveal oneself as one really is. It implies caring for each other and is a means of combating the essential loneliness of man. To be able to be intimate with another means giving up protective defenses which hide the reality about a person not only from others but from oneself.

An intimate relationship implies that all who are part of the relationship reveal themselves. In most psychotherapy, the therapist knows the individual or the group members intimately; but they do not know him. Existentialist therapists have challenged this position, believing that the intimacy of the "encounter" is the most potent force in treatment, that the capacity to be "real" in relationships is vital and, consequently, the therapist cannot remain aloof.

The following conditions are necessary for the establishment of intimacy: face-to-face interaction; willingness to take the risk of self-exposure; desire for closeness; a mutual demand for reciprocity; mutual attraction; trust and some degree of predictability; willingness to listen to and respond to the needs of others. Because of these conditions, the larger the group, the harder it becomes to establish a climate of intimacy.

Trust implies an expectation from the other. When a person trusts another, he makes a demand on him to respond in a particular way. There is confidence in the predictability of the other, an anticipation that the other will respond in terms of the demand, and a belief in the other's consistency. Trust is justified to the extent that the individual is capable of perceiving the reality of the situation. Trust can exist without mutual trust. There are degrees of trust related to the degree to which an individual feels justified in lowering his defenses. Trust involves risk-taking. It is probable that human beings start with a condition of confidence that their demands on others will be met. The degree to which this confidence in others continues is a matter of life experience and capacity to adapt to reality. Disillusionment is the result of trusting unrealistically, having expectations, and making demands on others which are not justified.

Termination of the Group

As the group moves toward the end of its life, termination maneuvers are undertaken. Members must withdraw from the group and assume their separate identities. They must now live independently. There are anxieties and feelings of loss. It is as if a part of oneself dies. A world ends. To soften the blow and delay the process, members review the past and project themselves into the future, both in words and action. They may relive incidents in the group. They will react to anxiety in their own typical fashion. The anticipated duration of the group will affect the speed of its formation and process. The frequency of exposure will also be a determining factor on the intensity of the group interaction.

Group Properties

As has been stated, groups can be studied at a number of different levels and from different points of view. Groups take place in various settings. They are of different sizes. They are organized differently. All these factors have implications for the way the group functions and what it can achieve.

To a great extent, what can be undertaken in any group is limited by what the community will tolerate. If a society does not permit open discussion of sex, no group run by a formal institution can adequately deal with this subject. The standing of the group in the open community will influence the attitudes which members have toward their groups. The same is true of the relationship between the institution and the group. The rules of the institution set the outer boundaries of the group. Its function and entry regulations will determine the population which it is possible to accept into the group. In general, a group which has high status in the community and in the institution will find it easier to obtain members. If a series of groups is to be undertaken, then the success of the first group is important. If there is conflict and confusion of role between the group leader and the staff of the institution, then the members in the group will be thrown into conflict. If there is conflict between the values held by the group and those of the members' other primary reference groups, the individual, in adopting the group's values, will distance and alienate himself from his other intimate associations and may be presented with a choice between them and the group—an important factor in the treatment of delinquent youth.

The Physical Environment

The immediate environment of the group affects its climate. The amount of space can limit the size of the group. If there is too much space, members may experience feelings of insignificance, emptiness, and anxiety. If there is too little, they may feel cramped and confined or too close together for their present state of intimacy. The proportions of the room and its color and cleanliness add to or detract from the free atmosphere of the group. Whether the group has privacy and can always have the room for itself affects what can go on in the sessions and indicates the respect with which the group is held by the institution.

The arrangement of the room and the spatial relationships of members to each other influence the functioning of the group. Because it is easier to talk when members look at each other, interaction is more spontaneous and member participation more general when groups are face to face. Rows of chairs may be satisfactory if communication is planned only between the leader and the group members; but if all are to join in freely, a circle makes interchange easier. A circle has another advantage over an oblong arrangement, for in the latter there are status positions which stimulate the development of hierarchy, whereas in a circle there is no predetermined leadership position. Participation is usually greater between members seated directly opposite each other rather than between those who are on the same side or segment of the oblong or circle. Positions also acquire emotional significance. A member who habitually seats himself opposite the leader is often competing for the leader's position. A member who sits next to the leader may be hiding from him or sitting next to him to gain support. The presence or absence of a table around which people sit can make a difference. The table is a protection or a barrier, and an empty space may create anxiety or stimulate closeness.

Size of the Group

Space and the size of groups are very closely related. Hall [4] has demonstrated that people in different cultures transact different kinds of operations at varying distances from each other. This seems to be part of the reason why a large group seems to have more difficulty in becoming intimate. A second reason is that the more people in a group the harder it is to get to know everyone well. Size also affects the amount of attention members can obtain from the group as a whole, from other members in the group, or from the leader. Some numbers of people have special properties. For instance, Simmel [5] and others have pointed out the tendency of groups of three to split into two against one. In very small groups, it is sometimes harder to maintain sufficient interest, excitement, and interaction. If there is an odd number, someone will have power to influence the decision between competing factions.

Member Participation

Participation of members in the group, as we have noted, is influenced by the seating arrangements and by the size of the group. It is also influenced by the way the leader, if there is one, conducts the group and by the composition of the membership. Vertical participation takes place between the leader and the

[4] Hall, *The Silent Language.*
[5] Wolff, *The Sociology of Georg Simmel.*

group as in a lecture; horizontal participation when members interact freely with each other. The more the leader takes responsibility for structuring group interactions and the more actively he leads, the more the group tends to interact vertically. The more members feel generally responsible for the group, the more likely they are to relate freely to each other. Sometimes a group will allow a member to monopolize the attention of the group for long periods of time or permit two people to "pair" and transact their business together while the rest of the group sits back and watches. These are often resistances to the performance of the group tasks.

Borgatta and Bales [6] have found experimentally that persons who are naturally low participators are more responsive in groups of low and medium participators and that they find it hard to become active in groups of fast reactors and highly aggressive participators.

Communication

Communication has been defined by Schachter [7] as "influence," that is, in simplest form, a stimulus which is sent out and has an effect on a receptor. This, of course, is then elaborated: stimuli sent to several receptors—stimulus, reaction, and response; stimulation of a chain or network of such interactions.

Ease of communication in small groups is affected by many factors:

1. Spatial factors, as has already been discussed; the distance between sender and receiver and their relative positions in the group;
2. Interference of competing noise or interruptions;
3. The quality and comprehensiveness of communication;

---

[6] Borgatta and Bales, "Interaction of Individuals in Reconstituted Groups," *Sociometry*, XVI (1953), 302–20.

[7] Schachter, "Deviation, Rejection, and Communication," in *Group Dynamics—Research and Theory*, eds. Cartwright and Zander.

4. Communication sets—differences in language and manner; differences in tone, expression, accent. For example: in culturally and intellectually mixed groups, those who talk in intellectual language need to try and make things simpler and more concrete and may need to learn street slang. Those who communicate in street talk may need to modify their language so that others understand. Both can help each other.

5. Restrictions which are placed on communication either in terms of direction (communication which has to go through certain channels), or in terms of subject matter or form;

6. Roles and positions which interfere with free communication; certain statements may carry penalties; rewards may be placed on adherence to certain forms of speech or certain psychological attitudes.

Communication may be verbal or non-verbal:

Non-verbal communication is conveyed by means of gestures, involuntary movements, changes in tension, breathing, expressions, and other ways.

Verbal communication relates to different kinds of language styles, ways of talking, speed and intonation, grammar, vocabulary, slang, and dialect. Both are connected to people's perception of themselves.

Although we are generally unaware of the preponderance of non-verbal communication, Birdwhistell estimates that not more than 10 per cent of all communication takes place through speech. Problems in communication are created by inconsistencies in verbal messages and between verbal and non-verbal communication, most well known in the "double-bind," in which contradictory instructions are conveyed in the same message.

Every culture has ritualistic communication sets used to ease communication and allay anxiety. Berne[8] has also identified

---

8 Berne, *Games People Play.*

and described typical transactions between individuals, which he calls "games," in which a cue will set off a typical series of predictable interactions, very frequently detrimental to the goals of the individuals. Groups are useful places in which to observe and identify such games.

The efficiency of communication is affected by the nature of the task, the positions of the communicators, the availability of information and feedback, the consistency of the messages and cues, and the receptiveness of the communicators. This last quality is affected by the emotional level of the leaders and receivers and the climate within which the communication takes place; the status and previous value sets of the parties; the degrees of information held; the relevance of the message for the receiver; the degree to which the communicators accept their roles; the amount of exposure to the messages and the setting in which the transaction takes place.

Leadership

Groups may have more or less formal structure. Leaders and officers may be appointed or elected into official roles, or leadership may develop spontaneously from the group and fluctuate in time. There is likely to be less stability of leadership in natural and informal groups than in highly structured ones. However, leaders must have support even to occupy a position of leadership, whether active leadership is performed or not. Leaders can be supported by their institutions or superiors, by wellplaced lieutenants, or by the general consent of the group or population. In order to be effective, leaders must possess power, either in the form of force or coercion or through being in tune with the demands and needs of the membership. The effectiveness of the leader is related to the relative strengths and weaknesses of the leader and the group. Unless the leader has, or can generate, very powerful support, he cannot afford to deviate too far from the norms of the group or he will be rejected by the members. Leaders may be attractive because they can serve the membership or because they represent what the people would like to do or be themselves. Thus, while leaders can deviate from the norms, they should embody the needs of the people they serve.

There are no typical leaders. Persons who are leaders in one group may not be accepted as such in another, and leadership functions will vary in different groups.

Some of the functions of leadership are: to bring membership together; to help the group identify its goals; to teach the group how to function; to help the group keep to the task; to serve as a model for the group; to present a value system to the group.

Leadership activities may include: stimulating interaction; making suggestions; providing for the needs of the group; seeing that the ground rules are set; influencing goals of the group; keeping order; assigning tasks; planning for or with the group; deciding upon membership; initiating action; evaluating the group.

The more active the leader is, and the more he takes over the responsibility for the group, the more dependent or defiant the group members are likely to become. In groups of immature members, when increased maturity is a goal, the leader must help the group set limits and structure which will allow the members to take maximum self-responsibility within those limits.

The more inactive a leader is and the less structure he establishes, the more a group is likely to function at a dynamic, emotional level unrelated to its stated objectives. The leader is a crucial influence on the tone of the group and the way it functions. Leaders vary in the amount of authority vested in them from external or internal sources and the degree to which they delegate authority to the group. If a leader delegates authority to the group for decision-making and then withdraws this authority, he is likely to create a climate in which members will be discontented and will conspire against him.

Realistic *decision-making* is based on:

1. The reality of alternatives and adequate consideration of probabilities.
2. Information about alternatives and hypotheses about consequences;
3. The prospect of implementing decisions.
4. The process in effective decision-making is to lay out the information, consider the alternatives, consider the implications, examine the desires and feelings of participants in the decision, and work out a course of action which is compatible with the goals of the members. In most real-life situations, decisions are made on predictions of outcome based on estimated probabilities.
5. Decisions in groups are made not only on the basis of information but on the alignment of forces.
6. Decisions are made through the balance between the two forces shifting to one side; decisions may be reversed when the balance of power changes within the group. When there is insufficient information, insufficient power to move the group in a particular direction, equal balance of opinion between members or uncertainty of members, no decision will be made.
7. Decisions will be influenced by previous experiences;
8. Decisions will be affected by the prospect of rewards or sanctions.
9. Lewin [9] demonstrated that the more people are involved and participate in discussion, the more likely they are to carry out the decisions.
10. Festinger [10] demonstrated that the harder it is to make

[9] Lewin, *Resolving Social Conflicts.*
[10] Festinger, "Group Attraction and Membership," *Journal of Social Issues,* VII (1951), 152–63.

a decision, the more an individual is likely to stay with it. However, in some very painful decisions, there is a tendency to regret decisions as soon as they are made; for example, divorce, hospitalization, adoptions. Possibly in all situations of pressure where decisions are made to relieve pressure, when this is achieved the unpleasant is forgotten, the pleasant remembered, and regret and desire to reverse the decision sets in.

11. There is a relationship between the motivations of members and decision-making: if individuals care very little or very much whether a decision is made, it may be easily made.

12. Decisions are related to value systems; if the permissible alternatives fall within the individual's or the group's interests, it will be easier to reach a decision than if they do not.

13. Structure and hierarchy can facilitate decision-making and task completion, particularly in the short-term group.

14. If the group members already have formed relationships with each other, it will be easier to come to a decision.

15. The boundaries and dimensions of decision-making in groups include:

   i. Who can participate in making a decision—in an advisory capacity or in actually making decisions?
      a. The leader may make the decision
      b. Several influential members may make it
      c. All members may participate

  ii. The structure of decision-making—formal voting or informal agreement—or decision by default;

 iii. The more the leader makes decisions, the more dependency he fosters in group members; if a change is made from leader to group decision-making, hostility will be the first reaction and an attack on the leader may follow;

iv. If leaders delegate decision-making power to the group, it is important that the group understand the limitations of that delegation and that their decisions hold good within these boundaries; in committees, the chairman is an important figure in decision-making—he can make sure who has the floor. He has a casting vote. He is in a position to stimulate certain suggestions from the members. He arranges the time when a decision has to be made. Groups vary in the degree to which the members involve themselves in decision-making and in the emphasis placed on decisions made by individuals in a group or on group decisions.

The Individual and His Role

A social role is a prescribed pattern of behavior related to a particular position in a social group. Role is concerned with function and position within the structure of a group. People function in a group in terms of their perceived roles.

In formal organizations, roles may be clearly defined. In informal groups or fluid situations, there may be *role conflict* between the needs of the situation, the expectations of others, and the view the group member has of his own role. However, even in well-established organizations where positions, jobs, and responsibilities are quite clearly defined, there may be marginal areas of conflict. For example, studies have shown that in hospitals there are frequent disparities between how nurses and doctors view their respective roles. (Stanton and Schwartz) [11]

In new and changing organizations, there is frequently considerable role confusion with consequent dislocation of functioning, conflict between individuals, and poor communication.

[11] Stanton and Schwartz, *The Mental Hospital.*

When there is considerable social or institutional change, people may find that the roles they were accustomed to play are no longer relevant. Individuals may play a number of different roles in different social groups, and in time an individual's role may change in a particular group. Changing roles may be the result of a change in the individual's own perception of what roles he should play, the pressure of other members, or the changing demands of the situation. The roles individuals accept will relate to their perception of themselves, their self-image or self-concept of their own identity, their personal goals, and to the opportunities and range of positions open to them. An individual's self-concept is his view of himself; how he should walk, dress, speak; how he feels about himself, whether he is stupid, clever, attractive, ugly; what kind of role he expects to play under a variety of circumstances. Changes in any one of these has implications for his view of himself and may threaten the individual's sense of identity with consequent anxiety and conflict.

The formation of the self-concept and the individual's perception of role possibilities are influenced by the innate capacities with which he is endowed, the culture in which he finds himself, his primary group mores and the changing environment he encounters, and the significant persons with whom he identifies. Individuals develop role conflict when they move into social groups with different demands, as when a small-town girl who still accepts the strict moral standards under which she has been brought up moves into a big-town social group where the standards for full acceptance into the group are very different.

Role flexibility. The capacity to play a number of different social roles with ease.

Role reversal. When individuals exchange roles or when an individual plays two opposing roles in different situations or at different times, as in some marriages when persons in time exchange roles in terms of dominance.

Stereotyping is the attribution of certain actions or functions to certain positions irrespective of their appropriateness or relevance. Stereotyping is frequent in marriage where there are certain cultural expectations with regard to the male and female roles. Each partner also brings his role expectations born of his life experiences, particularly in his own family. Early married life is a period during which the couple must accommodate their role expectations and work out more realistic roles which are more or less mutually satisfying, if the marriage is to endure. An individual becomes stereotyped in groups so that his actions are viewed in terms of his customary role rather than critically evaluated. It is sometimes hard to change others' expectations of oneself.

When an individual tends to play the same kind of role in a number of groups—such as a leadership role, a passive role, the role of an instigator, coercer, provocateur, an isolate, a scapegoat, or a clown—he is said to be consistent in his role. Roles have specific functions in the group; for example:

The clown. Clowning is defined as being funny through making oneself look clumsy, stupid, or silly. Clowning always involves drawing attention to oneself. It is an attempt to make others laugh. Purposes in clowning may be: to disguise one's feelings of incompetence or lack of social ease; to relieve tension; to subtly derogate others in situations where one's lack of competence also reflects other persons' ability to control the situation.

The scapegoat. Scapegoating is defined as the displacement of a group's anger onto one individual or group who may be inside or outside the main group. Conditions for scapegoating include a high level of tension (anger, anxiety, guilt, frustration); a person or section of the group against whom the members could rightly feel angry but for one reason or another are not able to express it, and a group or member who is seen as different, vulnerable, and open to attack. Such an individual usually arouses some irritation in his own right by provocativeness, high anxiety, irritating mannerisms, or superiority. Such individuals are typically those who imply that they know more than the rest or are more virtuous, or who possess more and flaunt their fortune, who have very different interests and do not accept the values of the group, or who are the sickest or the weakest. The scapegoat may be victimized, ostracized, or run out of the group.

Levels of Group Study

Groups can be considered in terms of the content on which members are concentrated. Themes can be isolated or the degree to which the overt tasks of the group are achieved can be evaluated. Formal and informal hierarchies, cliques, and member roles can be examined. Attempts can be made to analyze the underlying individual or group defensive structures. Groups can be considered in terms of the interaction between the member and the group or the group and the outer world. Lewin [12] originated the concept of "field" as the area in which interaction takes place. He was concerned with the examination of tension within this field. He described the prevailing atmosphere of the group as "the climate," was concerned with the relationship of any particular "field" to the total life space of the individuals, life space being all the fields within which an individual plays a part. He conceived that while a field was the area of immediate interaction, many other fields were related to the center of action in ghostly fashion through the lives of the individual members. An individual brings his significant relationships with him into any new interaction.

Lewin [13] and his school have been interested too in the positive and negative attractions or "valences" which constantly occur in groups; the power struggles resulting from these tensions and the whole dimension of control.

[12] Lewin, *Field Theory in Social Science.*
[13] Lewin, *Resolving Social Conflicts.*

Before turning to a consideration of ways in which groups are studied, it is important to consider the concept of the primary reference group first described by Hyman.[14] Primary reference groups are the most significant face-to-face cultural groups which influence the individual in forming his standards, values, and customary ways of behaving; most notably the family and the peer group. Any new group may become a reference for the individual, and the pressure of the group may influence him to change his standards and behavior.

Groups can be studied by direct observation or analysis of content of discussion or by obtaining information from those who have taken part in them. They can be studied in terms of their structure, that is, member participation and positioning, member roles and alliances; their overt content; the forces and maneuvers prevalent in the group, individual or group dynamics; the group process, changes in various dimensions over time.

Whether we are studying a group to observe and understand its operations or whether we are studying its efficiency in achieving certain goals, it is essential to conceptualize our purposes and to select the variables or dimensions which we plan to study. All the data or samples can be used.

Groups can be observed in a number of different ways:

Observers can be (1) participants; (2) inactive within the group; (3) outside the group, as behind a one-way mirror. Organizationally, observers can be (1) group members; (2) part of an interventionist team; (3) independent evaluators.

Problems in *observer reliability* are threefold: perceptual; emotional involvement and bias; and mechanical—problems of recording and remembering. Trained observers are more reliable, but of course they are more confined in what they observe and how they observe it.

---

14 Hyman, "The Psychology of Status," *Archives of Psychology* (1942), No. 269.

While the group is functioning, *records* can be made in the following ways: films or taped recordings; shorthand or descriptive account of all or part of sessions; summaries of selected interaction; recording of interaction in terms of particular categories; checking particular events or interactions as they occur on a structured schedule; tracking of member participation.

Records collected after group meetings and related to the group process or to members' reactions to the group can be organized in the following ways: a processed recording of the group in which a participant writes down everything that he can remember in the order in which it occurred; a summary of the group events which essentially emphasizes particular values or dimensions; check lists related to group events; sociometric choices—questioning which seeks to identify roles and cliques, members' feelings about each other; Q-sorts of member roles; content analysis of primary data; ratings of group or member behavior; interviews or questionnaires related to individuals' feelings about the group or their impressions of what is going on.

Some of the difficulties in studying groups are: (a) Much of the most important data about what is going on at a dynamic level is inferential. It is usually not clearly understood even by participants; (b) Much communication is nonverbal and consequently hard to observe, retain, and validate; (c) It is often very difficult to know where a sequence of interaction begins and ends; (d) Many interventions are multi-directional; they may be ostensibly directed at one person, but may have real relevance for another member or the group as a whole.

A number of systems have been developed for the recording and study of groups. Some of the most well-known are the following:

Sociometric diagrams. Sociometric diagrams are made to show the positions of members within a group. They are constructed either from tracking participation or from asking group members to make choices as to the members with whom they would like to associate for different activities or to rate members in terms of their roles and capacities (Moreno).[15]

Bales Interaction Analysis (Bales).[16] A series of 12 categories with which all group action is recorded. The actor, direction of action, and the time sequence can be recorded. There is no way to measure segments of interaction. There have been many modifications of this system, primarily concerned with task-oriented groups. Some variations of this are those by Borgatta and Bales,[17] Ruesch and Bateson,[18] Mann.[19]

Hill and Hill Interaction Matrix. A matrix which has been developed to try and evaluate the effectiveness of treatment groups in terms of a particular therapeutic orientation. Assumptions are made that self understanding is important, consequently the focus should be on the person rather than the group; treatment involves change which implies uncertainty and risk-taking. People must be able to accept help from others, and a change in behavior is most likely to occur through a study of what is happening in the present rather than the past. Four dimensions are studied: content; interpersonal interaction; willingness to work on problems; work style. Groups are evaluated for their effectiveness along these dimensions in terms of the theoretical orientation. For example, a group which is dealing with an immediate problem of one of the members, in which people are evaluating themselves and intent on helping and seeking help, is rated higher than a group which is discussing group phenomena in a general way, talking to the group rather

15 Moreno, *Who Shall Survive?*

16 Bales, *Interaction Process Analysis.*

17 Borgatta and Bales, "Task and Accumulation of Experience as Factors in the Interaction of Small Groups," *Sociometry,* XVI (1953), 239–52.

18 Ruesch and Bateson, *Communication, the Social Matrix of Psychiatry.*

19 Mann, "Dimensions of Individual Performance in Small Groups under Task and Social-Emotional Conditions," *Journal of Abnormal and Social Psychology,* LXII (1961), 674–82.

than to each other and not focusing down, or a group which is intent on tracking down the historical origins of a person's problems in an intellectualized way rather than solving them. The authors claim that the matrix can be used to evaluate groups along these dimensions which may have different purposes and consequently where different values are placed on the dimensions (Hill and Hill).[20]

Leary's system attempts to deal with both the action and the response. His categorization is inferential and consequently requires a psychologically sophisticated person. He deals with dimensions such as managerial-autocratic, docile-dependent (Leary).[21]

Whitaker and Lieberman—focal conflicts. Whitaker and Lieberman hypothesize that a group at any particular time is concerned with certain problems at an emotional and dynamic level. They attempt to identify these "focal conflicts" and to select transcripts of interaction which illustrate the group's operations (Whitaker and Lieberman).[22]

Leader operations. A number of workers have concentrated on attempting to conceptualize the operations essential to the creation of certain kinds of group climates or the undertaking of certain group operations. The most famous of these is the study of authoritarian, democratic, and laissez-faire groups by Lippitt and White.[23]

[20] Hill and Hill, *Interaction Matrix* (*HIM*).

[21] Leary, *The Interpersonal Diagnosis of Personality.*

[22] Whitaker and Lieberman, *Psychotherapy Through the Group Process.*

[23] Lippitt and White, "An Experimental Study of Leadership and Group Life," in *Readings in Social Psychology,* ed. T. M. Newcomb.

III

The Adolescent and His Culture

Adolescence

Before we start to work with adolescents, it is important for us to consider the nature of adolescence itself. Each stage of life has special tasks and intrinsic problems with which its members have to deal. Adolescence is a period of great change which marks the transition from childhood to adult life. During this time boys and girls have to establish their identities as men and women; to decide what kinds of roles they wish to play in the adult world socially, sexually, and occupationally; to separate themselves from their primary families, to become independent and to envisage the establishment of their own families.

Sometime between the age of 10 and 14 years all boys and girls begin to experience physical changes which increase their awareness of sexual differentiation. For the first time in their lives they really begin to see themselves and are seen by their parents and other adults as potential young men and women. There is a great deal of self-consciousness about one's body and appearance, and the youngsters begin to be preoccupied with their individual and sexual identity.

They match themselves against and are curious about members of their own sex. There is much experimentation with different syles of living, dress, walk, and speech. They are identified strongly with each other, compete strongly against each other, want to be together a great deal of the time. Implicitly, they seem to be asking "what is it like to be a man? (or a woman?)" In this period of early adolescence there is relatively little interest in the opposite sex as people. Where sexual interest is present it confirms one's own power to attract or confirms one's own inadequacy. Instinctual drives begin to be strong but are not well channeled, so that they are expressed in fluid anxiety and mood swings. There is a great deal of self doubt and preoccupation with one's self, and self esteem is precarious. There is a reluctance to admit to any problem, but often a fluctuation between extreme reticence and idealistic verbosity, or on the other hand much use of physical activity to handle anxiety. Along with explorations of identity, there is also an exploration of values and an overvaluation of what is new and different.

At this time there is also an increase in the intensity of the desire to be both dependent and independent, a need for autonomy and at the same time a need for the security of being able to fall back and depend on adults when life is difficult. There is at times a need to renege on responsibility. Thus, antiauthoritarianism and defiance are very easy to arouse.

As the boys and girls begin to think of being adult, they also have to begin to face the question of what kinds of lives they will lead when they grow up. For many this can be an occasion for panic or despair. Many children from lower-class backgrounds do not have any prospect of a bright future. Children from all walks of life can be afraid about the need to commit themselves to a career or to a marriage and the thought of being a parent.

This prospect of becoming adult and the changed perception of the adolescent which both youth and the adults experience can arouse much confusion and anxiety. Parents and children suddenly find each other attractive. In close families this can engender panic. In a different way, this can also make for difficulty at school and other settings where boys suddenly become very sensitive of their maleness with female teachers, girls become provocative with their male teachers, and where the intensity of identification with members of one's own sex becomes a factor in the adolescent "crush."

In the group, boys and girls are typically restless. Conversation is often diffuse, confused, and diversionary. There is much giggling, touching, horseplay, getting up, walking around. Attention span is brief and the ability to stay with anxiety-provoking topics is limited. Group members struggle for a while, then move away into gossip or physical activity.

The young adolescent tests out his potentialities sexually, socially, and occupationally, but to a great extent in terms of his present feelings about himself. Somewhere between 15 and 18 years the growing up process begins to be dealt with at a level more related to future life. The adolescent begins to face in earnest the decisions he must make about the adult role which he will play in his work and social life; to make an occupational choice; to deal with the need to separate realistically from his parents and become independent; to know the opposite sex more intimately, and to think about selecting a mate and establishing one's own family. The intense interest in the same sex, which is typical of early adolescence, is subdued into comradeship or a competitive relationship. In this later stage, the individual tends to be more stable and gradually acquires an increased ability to deal with the opposite sex, to make some decisions about how one will manage sexual relations and conform to the mating customs of one's group. Although the problems around identity are still considerable, they are expressed less generally in terms of what it is like to be a man or a woman, but more specifically in terms of what kind of man or woman one wants to be, what role one is going to play, and how one is going to relate to the opposite sex.

It is easier for adolescents in this later stage to admit that they have problems and are concerned about themselves. They are more generally willing to accept help and are able to sustain focused discussions for much longer periods. Ideally, as the adolescent reaches maturity, there should be less tendency to fluctuate between dependency and independence, less emotionality and more capacity to maintain one's self as an independent adult, and more responsibility for planning one's life and carrying out one's plans. In general, boys and girls tend to become less impulsive and more able to express themselves in words rather than physical behavior.

Because boys and girls are re-examining their standards and values during adolescence, taking stock of themselves, thinking through what kind of adult lives they are going to try for, and because at the same time they are rejecting earlier standards and with these, frequently, all significant adults in their first rebellion against childishness and dependency, the peer group becomes extremely important. It forms for the adolescents an important reference group through which they can work out new standards, confirm their identities, gain support and security, and satisfy dependency needs without surrendering their new found independence. Through the group they can gain status and a feeling of belonging. Peer groups form a very important defense against feelings of loss of identity and alienation which can be harmful in adolescence. Essentially, for many boys and girls who find it difficult to gain a place in regular society, who because of social or psychological difficulties or economic deprivation do not feel that they are part of the favored and valued groups where opportunities are rife, the delinquent gang performs this function of being, as a deviant reference group, a mainstay in their lives.

The concept of reference groups is also important as a means of changing behavior. Counseling groups and therapy groups are essentially new reference groups, which create their own standards and values and ways of behaving, which exert pressure on all to conform, and which throw the individual group member into conflict between his old ways and the new. The willingness of any individual to adopt a new reference group is always closely related to the way in which he sees himself. It is clearly also true that when an individual adopts a new reference group, some changes will occur in his own self image and in his relationship to his old way of life.

Some of the important tasks which face adolescents in general are (1) to obtain some clear idea about the kind of persons they want to be and what kinds of roles they are going to play in life, to be able to take responsibility for themselves, and to plan and carry out those plans; (2) to sort out their own feelings about what is expected of men and women and how they will get along with their own and the opposite sex; (3) to develop a self image which they themselves can respect; (4) to learn to understand human interaction and to respond appropriately; (5) to understand the structure and functioning of the world around them and to be able to assess opportunity realistically; (6) to think through and work out for themselves their own standards and values; (7) to be willing to involve themselves with others and to help them and to receive help; (8) to allow themselves to feel and to risk expressing what they feel when it's appropriate; (9) to be able to mobilize their energies to action. More specifically, during adolescence boys and girls have to choose and begin to train for adult occupations; they have to prepare themselves for marriage and parenthood; to come to terms with themselves as men and women and to learn how to mate, to separate themselves from their families, and to take on adult responsibility. Early adolescence is concerned primarily with the establishment of a sexual identity and beginning to come to terms with an independent life, and late adolescence is concerned with the actual separation from the family and the making of mating and occupational choices.

The Culture

The forces which impinge on the boy or girl during adolescence vary considerably depending on his cultural position, and the custom of studying the adolescent only in terms of his physical or psychological growth and development has in recent years been modified to include the socio-cultural analysis of the field in which his personality has developed. In order to assist young people to grow to maturity we need to understand the economic, social, and cultural background.

Since it is impossible in a study of this type to go into all the possible cultural implications of class, race, religion, neighborhood, family, and age groups, we will limit ourselves to certain general categories and the questions that they raise pertinent to our purpose.

In our work with groups, we need to know what life-styles and values an adolescent brings to the group associations and outlook. Life style is the pattern of behavior which results from an accumulated psychological and cultural heritage. It is observable and lends itself to study. Efforts directed at rehabilitation will involve changes in life styles. Efforts directed at socialization should increase the range of adaptions within a life style.

The problems of growing up are exacerbated in modern society because there are few really meaningful roles for adolescents. Adults tend to distrust the young, to consider them irresponsible and to fear their competition. Many restrictions may be placed on the adolescent. He may not be allowed to work, to earn money, or to leave home. He consequently cannot become independent. He cannot marry and assume family responsibilities before a certain age. He may not even be allowed to move freely in the community after dark, enter certain places of entertainment, or drive a car because his behavior is suspect. It may well be necessary for us to work to change the environment as well as to reinforce the youth's natural inclination toward maturity. Group counselors and therapists need to develop an awareness of what effect their own group identification and values have on teen-agers who might come from similar or radically disparate backgrounds.

We can speak of youth and their families as being economically, socially, culturally, or educationally deprived. Recent discussions on the economically deprived have tended to lump all of these categories together under that banner, thereby causing confusion and some resentment from those whose backgrounds are, or were at one time, economically, but not necessarily otherwise, deprived. Likewise, there has been an understandable hesitance to particularize the deprivation factors, as they are seen today to be so closely interrelated among the population which remains at the bottom of the ladder. For our purposes, it is necessary to view these factors separately so that we may better comprehend what adolescents bring to groups and what effects the groups will have on them.

The economic category is the easiest to delineate. "Poor" means insufficient earnings to adequately feed, house, and clothe according to basic minimal standards. Up-to-date figures on individual and family needs are available through government statistical studies. If we know what the family income is and how many have to live on it, we can learn whether a youth comes from a destitute, poor, marginal, adequate, or comfortable economic situation relative to the city or area in which he lives. Next we can attempt to find out how many day or nighttime hours either or both parents work to earn that income and what sort of work is done for the money being earned.

At this point we begin to move into social and cultural areas. Is this work which is above or beneath the educational or training level of the adult in the family? Is it "clean" work or "dirty" work? Is it work done with pride or disgust? What does the youth know about his mother's or father's work? From this information, added to a general impression of the meaning of work in his community, we might draw some hypotheses about attitudes toward the value of education and training and the learning about work habits within the family. As we go along, we get into areas that are just as pertinent to questions about the middle-class youth. A father who is a successful business-man might convey a cynical attitude about labor. A tolerant attitude about cheating can be conveyed or encouraged in any family. Attitudes about competition are relevant, particularly in the middle classes where subtle contradictions are often apparent.

We might ask questions about the rent a family pays and what they get for this rent in living space and utilities. Do they pay more rent for poorer housing because of discrimination in the community? Is heat included in the rent, or will the family become very hard up in the winter because it must pay for its own heat, a practice not unknown in the slum areas of some cities.

Living space is closely related in its meaning to the numbers, ages, and sexes of those sharing the space. It is not uncommon for more than one "family" to share an apartment or rooms in an urban slum.

What do you mean by "family" when we ask this question? We must find out "who lives in your home?" Where they sleep? In how many beds? In what combinations and at what times? Are there opportunities for physical privacy?

We are now exploring areas potentially loaded with feelings for the adolescent. Let us imagine the "worst" possible set of circumstances: a family or the extension thereof, in which there are no opportunities for privacy nor any inclination for adults to manage their sexual conduct away from the view of younger members of the household. Perhaps, too, there are not enough beds so that adolescents of different sexes are sharing the same bed. Also, the mother has not one man, but a series of men; and some of these are indiscriminate and force themselves on the adolescent females in the household. Here is a situation in which there is no protection for the teen-ager. Precocious sexual activity has not necessarily been encouraged, but nothing has been done to actively prevent it from taking place.

How one conducts a discussion with a group of teen-agers on the subject of sex depends very much on the background of the teen-ager. Boys and girls living in the slums have often had considerable sexual experience at an early age, while some middle-class children are ignorant even of the facts of life. Diagnostic studies of youth brought to child guidance clinics for learning problems and other anxiety reactions of childhood have uncovered a general failure on the part of middle-class parents to guard the privacy of their own bodies. Bed hopping is tolerated, co-ed baths thought instructional. Questions asked by children about sex are injudiciously answered in advance of the child's "need to know." Therapy with these children has shown that these "open" practices are anxiety producing and frequently debilitating. Yet parent after parent is confused and hurt when this is pointed out, because somehow the impression that openness was an antidote to suppression had been conveyed by popularized psychological studies.

We should try to learn something about eating customs. Does the family eat together? If not, who sits down with whom and who doesn't sit down? Why don't they? A poor mother might not sit down because there aren't enough chairs or table utensils, a middle class mother because she has become the anxious conveyor of food between the pot and her children's mouths.

How about responsibility? Too often youth from economically deprived homes appear to be irresponsible, when in actuality they are rebelling against premature, inappropriate, and overwhelming responsibilities for the care of younger siblings and household while the mother is out scraping a living with which to feed and house her brood. The middle-class youth might be irresponsible too, but for a different reason. Not recognizing the need for growing independence in adolescents is a familiar problem in many middle-class families, and as a consequence little provision is made for the gradual assumption of adult responsibilities in the family economy.

Who does the mothering, and who the fathering? The standard American middle-class pattern has been for a mother and father to establish a household for themselves and their offspring, the father working to support the household, the mother organizing it while caring for their children. Grandparents live in their own homes and hopefully do not interfere. The varieties of this pattern are almost impossible to enumerate. Increasing numbers of middle-class mothers are working while their children are cared for by paid mother substitutes.

The problem of the mother surrogate and the transmittal of socialization patterns, although different in both classes, needs further study. Poor mothers work while children are cared for by grandmothers, by older siblings who, in desperation, are kept home from school, or by still older siblings who have dropped out of school and are unemployed. The children might be "carried" to a neighbor's house and some money paid for the care of the child from the mother's meager earnings. A child may have cared for himself from after school until suppertime ever since the start of his school years.

Are the parents divorced, separated, or was there never a marriage? If so, what attitudes and patterns flow from a family situation in which a male authority figure is missing or changes frequently? And in the eyes of the adolescent males of the household, what authority has a man living at home who is unemployed—not treated respectfully by wife or by such community authorities as police or welfare personnel? [1] And in the family where a male authority is missing, is the situation compounded by the virtual absence of male teachers in the elementary grades?

Another question related to mothering and fathering has to do with the degree of supervision and protection offered the adolescent as he moves from a more dependent position in the

[1] Lee Rainwater discusses some of the implications of the changing male figure in an excellent article on Negro identity in *Daedulus* (special issue, Winter, 1966), Vol. 94 (5).

family toward a greater assumption of responsibility for his own care and behavior. In many middle-class families, parents are afraid to allow their children to experiment and make mistakes and have difficulty in trusting them. However, opportunities for a satisfying development are available frequently from other sources, such as schools and clubs, if the adolescent can mobilize himself to take advantage of them.

On the other hand, the adolescent from a socially deprived background often has to face a different problem. He has had minimal support from his famliy and from latency age has had to turn mainly to his peers in the street. With this has come much opportunity for risk taking and experimentation. His problem is to sustain the environmental stresses to which he is subjected and to find a meaningful role with adequate opportunity which he can utilize in adult life. He usually has had poor experiences with adults and has little confidence in them. Basic feelings of inferiority and despair are often concealed beneath a rebellious front.

Social deprivation may be said to apply to a situation where the immediate family resources are inadequate, the larger community is seen as hostile, and, at the same time, no social institutions exist that can fill the gap. When large numbers of Jewish families migrated from Europe at the turn of the century, they were frequently impoverished, could not speak the language, and saw America and its ostensibly open society as hostile in contrast to the protected life of the European Jewish community or ghetto. What social institutions helped them to master this frightening situation, a situation not unlike that of the poor rural white or Negro arriving in a big city in an effort to better himself? A tradition of social organization long established to care for those in need, based on the family or the "landsman" from the same town in Europe, was probably equal in importance to the tradition of education of the young and the value placed on education for its own sake.

In the "neighborhood farm system" (Alissi),[2] is it good to be bad, or bad to be bad? Cut off as they are from any real contact with the broader community except through those institutions which are experienced as punitive (police, schools, welfare), do community members view delinquent behavior with stricture or leniency? Do the adolescents of this community imitate adults, as is commonly thought; or more subtly, do they act out the delinquent fantasies of these adults? Implications for work with these groups differ, depending on our view of these particular factors.

If we are trying to help adolescents change their ways, we must recognize that their efforts will be affected by their environment. Even though there may be some temporary upset in family dynamics when middle-class youth change, in general their socially acceptable adaptations will move them closer to the ideals and standards of their relatives, friends, and the community. Their primary groups will regard and reinforce progress as opportunities open up for them. This is not so true of low income youth, particularly those who are drawn from a delinquent subculture. With such youth, the move toward greater acceptance in the larger society may mean abandoning ways of life which are required by friends and family in the old world and consequent estrangement from them. The fact that changes in one element in an individual's life or in an institution or community may require alterations in many other factors has to be taken into consideration in planning intervention.

Vinter and Sarri [3] are concerned with this point when in the public school they propose that "malperformance patterns should be viewed as resultants of the interaction of both pupil characteristics and school conditions." In their study of five contrasting southeastern Michigan school systems, they found

---

[2] Alissi, "Social Influences on Group Values," *Social Work*, X (1965).
[3] Vinter and Sarri, "Malperformance in the Public School: A Group Work Approach," *Social Work*, X (1965).

significantly differing attitudes on the part of the school administrators toward academic failure and misbehavior. Some were able to particularize problems of adolescents with regard to school behavior while others generalized and presented double and triple penalties for youth who were not able to meet the expectations of the system. From their viewpoint, youth, teachers, and administrators must all interact and change in order to evolve a more efficient system.

Schools have been criticized for failing to comprehend the educational needs of the economically deprived and, at the same time, for short-changing them by expecting poor performance or presenting them with a merely vocational outlook. While undoubtedly requiring many changes, the schools have become a community scapegoat as we view society's failure to rehabilitate the deprived. Here too, it is necessary to ask some careful questions in regard to the adolescent we work with, be he affluent or poor. Questions related to parental and school pressures for academic achievement are relevant in affluent communities, while what is offered and what is expected in poorer neighborhood schools should be explored. The relationship between youth and the school—their effects on and expectations of each other—are important in any neighborhood.

Other areas that help us to understand the background of the adolescent and give us some clues about his value systems are:

1. How "open" or "closed" is the community he lives in? This will tell us something about his potential attitudes about "others," those of different economic backgrounds, races, religions.

2. What radio, television, newspaper, films, and other public communications media does he respond to? This will give us a clue to his "culture heroes," outlook, and wider frames of reference. We should also try to learn how much time he spends "passively absorbing." In many

culturally deprived homes the radio or television set are on almost constantly, leaving little chance for private quiet reflection or productive homework.

3. What language is spoken in the home? Is it adequate English, a foreign language, or a word-poor dialect? Are the patterns of verbal stimulus and response in the home active or passive? The implications here are many, particularly in relation to school and job performance. For years schools have been dealing with native American populations whose vocabulary and dialect preclude success at reading and even understanding the teacher. The effect on the adult responsible for any group, school, counseling, or therapy can be angry paralysis when he cannot understand or be understood by the group members, especially when both are ostensibly speaking the same language. Language styles also have implications for the kind of counseling or psychotherapy one undertakes. Many middle-class youth are highly verbal and avoid reality with words and abstractions. In a different way, low income youth may do the same thing by conning and "boxing in" operations, even though in general less educated youth work better in a setting which is concrete and closely related to real life.

Something needs to be said about the problem of emotional privacy, particularly in the enlightened middle-class home. Here, where the children are few and the energy of the parents directed so intensively toward "doing a good job," a special burden is placed on the children. This is caused by the drive of the parents to "communicate" with their children and to have everything explained. A demand is implicit or explicit that the child do his share, too, in telling the parent everything, allowing the parent to guide the child with advice and judgment. The process appears to be somewhat like "brainwashing." The healthy questioning and criticism of authority which should be a part of adolescence gives way to a variety of symptoms particular to our age. For some there is premature conformity. Other reactions are expressed by the beatnik, passively angry, unachieving, unallied with any cause and showing no sign of wanting to be an adult; the new young conservative seeking a return to the good old days; the hippie searching for personal meaning and intimacy. Most of these come from middle-class homes.

The problem of the role of women in our society has a bearing on the widespread lack of academic drive in older adolescent girls. There is a frequent drop in achievement when girls begin to concern themselves about the popular notion that "boys don't like bright girls." Yet, many women must provide for themselves and their children without assistance from a husband or other relatives. Dating is encouraged at earlier ages, although attitudes toward premarital sex are very confused and contraceptive protection generally withheld, with consequent unstable early marriages or illegitimate pregnancy. Discussions with high school classes and social groups in centers and churches frequently concern themselves with problems related to these areas.

Being raised in a female-based household has important implications for the personality of both male and female offspring. Since the sex-based division of labor generally found in the middle-class family (father—primary responsibility for obtaining basic income, minor domestic maintenance and repair tasks, purchase and maintenance of car; mother—primary responsibility for child care, purchase of food and material goods, food preparation, cleaning, entertaining) cannot be maintained in the female-based unit, the adult women must be able to engage in a set of activities and to some degree manifest attributes generally associated with the male in the "ideal" American family. The adolescent girl from a poor family frequently maintains close contact with a male street-corner group and goes through a period of attempting to model her behavior after that of the boys—adopting similar patterns in dress and language, with stress on the "masculine" qualities of toughness, fighting prowess, and "hardness." The adult women, in light of the undependable presence of the male in the household and the serial mating pattern, must be prepared to assume and reassume the roles of mate-seeker, mother, and employee in recurring succession, rather than as fairly distinct and nonrepetitive phases, as is so for most middle-class women. The necessity of being prepared to assume a mate-seeking role places the adult mother, in this respect, in competition with her adolescent daughter; and mother and daughter often relate to one another more as peers than as parent and child. The "peer" quality of the mother-daughter relationship also derives from the fact that older daughters must learn at an early age to assume aspects of the "mother" role for their younger siblings.

The boy raised in a female-based household faces problems of sex-role identification which have an important bearing on the emphasis of lower class male culture, the form and functions of the "gangs" or street-corner groups, and the nature and durability of adult mating patterns. The boy's mother, through her own life experience, generally regards men as unreliable and untrustworthy; the definition "all men are no good" is common. Sensing the impermanence and the lack of dependability of a marital relationship with an adult male, the mother focuses on her own son as a primary object of love and nurturance. In consequence, the mother-son relationship is one of great emotional significance, and probably the most important tie in such family constellations.[4] The mother strives to maintain a solitary relationship with her son and to prevent him from assuming attributes of the adult male which she perceives as "no good." This situation has several implications for the boy's personality. On

[4] Hollingshead, *Elmtown's Youth: The Impact of Social Classes on Adolescents.* Hollingshead reports that "The mother-child relationship is the strongest and most enduring tie," (p. 117) in the lower class community of a medium-sized midwestern city.

the one hand, he regards his relationship with his mother as "sacred," seldom derogating or condemning her openly, while frequently blaming or expressing hostility to "the old man." He ascribes his successes to her and regrets his transgressions primarily for her sake. On the other hand, the boy tends to internalize his mother's definition of men as "no good," and when, as an adult, he engages in the customary behavior patterns of his male peers, sees this as proof of his innate "weakness" or "badness," and in castigating himself will reflect the anticipated censure of his mother: "You turned out just like your father after all."

IV

General Considerations in Group Counseling and Group Psychotherapy

Just because the adolescent is generally in a state of re-examining his position in relation to the adult world, has fluctuating feelings toward adults, and is inclined to seek support, assistance, and confirmation of his judgment from his peers, groups are considered to be particularly useful in working with this age group. The group situation has advantages over individual treatment. Small groups provide a miniature real-life situation which can be utilized for the study and change of behavior. In groups, people expose their typical patterns of operation. New ways of dealing with situations can be learned in action. New skills in human relations can be developed, current problems resolved, standards and values re-examined and altered. The group, skillfully conducted, can provide a mirror in which the group member can evolve a new concept of himself, test this out in action with his fellows, and find new models for identification. Furthermore, when people get together in a group they lose a unique sense that they are the only ones who have problems. They feel less isolated. They can increase their self-esteem through their acceptance by the group and their ability to help others.

Groups are not necessarily positive, however. A group has to become an efficient functioning unit in order to become a potent force and be able to exert pressure on the individual to conform to the group's expectations. Thus, certain concepts are important for our approach to group counseling and group psychotherapy, whatever the level and goal of treatment.

First, life is not static. It is not possible to solve a problem and live happily ever after. Life is continuing change, and one's role in life changes over time, from infancy to childhood to adolescence, adulthood in society with formal responsibility, and finally an older person abdicating from some of these responsibilities. Every one must constantly face new situations, develop, adjust, adapt themselves, find new solutions to new problems.

Group members need help in thinking about what kinds of skills they must develop in order to obtain what they want out of life and to avoid trying to get what is not possible. In order to deal with life successfully, one has to learn to face problems and to cope with a variety of different situations. The greater one's range and efficiency, the more satisfactory one's life is likely to be.

A necessary attribute in counseling and therapy groups is the concept that people should help each other. This combats sibling rivalry and jealousy. It promotes the idea that there is enough for all—love, credit, gratification—and that satisfaction can come from helping each other obtain these. It promotes feelings of intimacy and trust, of interdependence, and develops the capacity to take responsibility for oneself and to accept responsibility toward others.

To take part in counseling and psychotherapy means to accept the need to change. While some few adolescents accept this readily, many do not; and this raises the question of motivation. Certainly, it is hard to see how change can occur unless there is contact and exposure to some change agent. Change in the individual is not likely to occur unless there is a change in the forces impinging on the individual or unless there is a change in the intrapsychic balance. It can be that when an individual experiences success his feelings about himself alter, he becomes more secure and is able to be more tolerant of others. It may be, however, that forces have to be created which present the individual with new dilemmas and militate new choices before any movement can take place.

A special problem with therapy groups is the need for the patient to admit inadequacies or the existence of problems. It becomes essential to promote an atmosphere in which problems are accepted as normal. In such a climate, it is all right to be wrong, provided one is willing to look at and learn from one's mistakes, and necessary to recognize that one cannot know everything or behave perfectly at all times. Failure is no longer a catastrophe, but an opportunity to learn and to try again. This means the development of an atmosphere of undefensiveness in groups, promoted by the leader's own attitudes. It implies further a tolerance and acceptance of oneself with all one's assets and liabilities, surrendering the need to be right, perfect, and omnipotent at all times.

Counselors and therapists must recognize that resistance is an intrinsic part of the struggle to change. If there were no conflict, there would be no need for the group or no hope that change could take place. Resistance is the sign that members are involved. The problem then is to mobilize forces constructively so that the group members can move ahead and work through their problems.

Adolescents may seek help or information. They may be exposed to new situations which upset earlier adjustments and with which they need help, or counseling may arise in the course of normal activities such as school, recreation, or job training.

Kinds of Groups

There has been much discussion about what counseling, psychotherapy, casework, therapeutic group work, and so on are. In our opinion, there is considerable overlap, and boundaries are unclear. However, there are two main dimensions. First, there is counseling which is considered a necessary part of normal living, such as vocational counseling and frank discussions on subjects of interest to teen-agers, or counseling which is built into normal activities, such as how to deal with a supervisor or how to make decisions in a playgroup. Then there is counseling which deals with behavior or situations which are considered pathological by society. This is called treatment, psychotherapy, or rehabilitation. Second, there are levels of group management and goals related to whether the environment has to be restructured, or whether specific changes in interpersonal relationships or in intrapsychic functioning have to made. Although there are different degrees of competence, education, and training related to different levels of group management which will be dealt with later, for purposes of simplification we will talk about group leaders in our general discussion and refer to group counseling as an all-emcompassing term.

Though many counseling groups are part of normal life, it has to be recognized that treatment groups, whether they are held in youth counseling centers, child guidance or psychiatric clinics, doctors' offices, schools, or courts, all carry the implication that the teenager needs help. He has to admit that there is something wrong with him since he is not realizing his potential and since he cannot change his situation by his own efforts alone. He must place himself in a dependent position to the therapist and submit to the ground rules of the treatment. He has to face the fact that he must change in order for the situation to be different. This is particularly hard for the teen-ager who already feels insecure and is striving to become autonomous and independent. Teen-agers attend these groups for one of three reasons: 1) they recognize that they need help and are willing to seek it out; 2) they obtain other kinds of gratification in the treatment; 3) they are forced to attend.

A very small proportion of adolescents are willing to admit openly that they need help. Many come because they attain some other gratification, such as the group is also fun, other activities are included, the group is heterosexual and stimulating, or the members become very attached to each other. Teen-agers may attend groups because their parents force them to, because the school insists that they attend as a condition of promotion or attendance, or because the court demands it. Institutional groups, of course, are very frequently captive audiences. The type of group will very much determine the selection of group members; and this in turn is related to the setting of the group, the role of the institution, and so on.

Thus, when we contemplate starting a group program, there are a number of factors which have to be taken into consideration.

1. How do we decide what kind of program should be established? How do we determine goals? What will be the group atmosphere? How will it function?
2. What is the population we are planning to serve, and what are their needs? How do we select and prepare members?
3. How large will the groups be, and how long will they last?
4. What is the function of the institution within which we are planning the program? What are its assets and limitations? How does the group program fit into the organization?
5. What resources do we have? Are they adequate? If not, can we obtain what we need in the way of personnel, space, supplies, and other needs?
6. What are the attitudes of all personnel within the institution to the program, and what roles will they have? What administrative structure needs to be set up?
7. How will the groups be related to other programs in the institution and in the community?

The Program and Population

Although occasionally programs are established to meet a demand to train personnel or because of special research interests, most group counseling and therapy programs are started to meet some need for service either in the community or in a particular institution. In a youth counseling agency, there may be a long waiting list, or many boys and girls may find it hard to respond to an individual contact, so groups are established to solve these problems. In the school, there may be a need for vocational counseling, sex education, or the management of learning and behavior problems. In employment agencies, group counseling may be seen as an aid in preparing youth for work. In all situations there must be a perceived need and a sufficient number of people who can be gathered into a group before a program can succeed.

The goals of the groups must, of course, be related to the needs of the population; and the selection of members, methods used, and duration of the groups will be determined by these goals.

If the needs are general to the community, a decision has to be made as to where the program will be housed. All settings have their advantages and disadvantages. Each institution carries its own image in the community. A school may be a pleasurable or neutral setting for many young people; but for the boy or girl who is in trouble or failing to learn, it has disagreeable connotations. For many such boys and girls, a counseling group in the school setting might well have to be made mandatory or the youngsters will not attend; and this will affect the management of the group. A psychiatric clinic can be thought of as a place for people who are crazy or queer, and always requires the patient to recognize that he has a need for help. A group in a recreation center is necessarily composed of members who come voluntarily and who expect to have fun and to enjoy the group.

Consequently, members may be captive, as in residential institutions or in schools. They may be enjoined to attend groups, as youngsters on probation sometimes are; or they may come in voluntary fashion either because they are invited to participate or because they apply.

In setting up groups, the size and availability of the population has to be taken into consideration. If a community psychiatric agency has only two girls in early adolescence who are applying for treatment, it may be hard to start a group for them. Case finding will have to be undertaken.

In school, decisions have to be made as to whether the groups will be conducted as classes, as special programs within school time, or as after-school clubs or counseling. Scheduling problems have to be taken into consideration.

Groups may be established with membership drawn from agency waiting lists. Members may be invited or assigned from existing agency populations, such as probation caseloads or school classes; or they may have to be specially recruited as when a clinic informs its sources of referral that it plans to start a particular kind of group and is ready to accept patients; or a recreation center announces a group program to which all interested may apply.

Goals

In all group programs there are general goals for the program, goals for each group, and expectations with regard to individuals in the group.

It is not enough to say, "We think groups are a great idea. Let's start a group." All groups are not beneficial. Delinquent boys who band together in a group and reaffirm their delinquent standards are not being helped to establish a socially acceptable way of life. Equally, a group which is very suitable for an anxious, shy, and constricted youngster may well be quite unsuitable for a sociopath who already has difficulty managing his impulses.

Program goals, as we have stated, are related to the preconceived needs of a population. Within a group program, a number of different kinds of groups may be set up.

Groups vary in the degree to which goals for individual members are differentiated. Major concern in some groups is to establish a particular kind of climate in which all will react. In others, there is consideration of specific problems. In some groups, these are common difficulties; in others, problems are unique to each member. For example, in a group for boys and girls who are learning to manage diabetes, a coma-free life will be a goal for all members. This may be a short-term group concentrating on the requirements of a diabetic life and the clarification of feelings and confusions about having to live such a life. However, a group for boys and girls who are having difficulty managing their lives so as to control their diabetes may move from the overt problem into many other aspects of their lives and to a consideration of more general patterns of adjustment, such as a need to be taken care of and to avoid responsibility for self or a sado-masochistic struggle which is continuous between parent and child. In these instances, goals for each member will become individualized; and treatment will need to be more intensive and will take much longer, for the focus will be on the maladjustment of the individual and in helping him change self-destructive patterns of behavior. It might well be that if we discovered such individuals in our short-term orientation group, we might prefer to discuss with them the more general consideration of how they managed their lives and to assign them to a treatment group composed of patients who were manifesting their basic difficulties through a variety of symptoms.

When we discuss setting goals for individuals, it has to be understood that this is related to the problems which have to be dealt with rather than the ultimate decisions. In the final analysis, only the individual can decide what he wants to do with his life. If he decides problems cannot be given up because they carry too much satisfaction as well as pain, or if he finally decides that he prefers to accept lesser goals, that is his prerogative. The task of the leader is to promote individual development, to assist the group in exploring situations, and to become knowledgeable and realistic enough to be able to make decisions which are responsible and satisfying to them.

Levels of Counseling

There are essentially four different levels within group counseling and group psychotherapy.

1. Groups which are set up primarily for information and orientation;
2. Groups concerned with specific problems and their resolution;
3. Groups related to general life adjustments demanding changes in self-concept and self-management;
4. Indirect counseling which arises out of other activities: play, clubs, skills and crafts groups, teaching and training settings, and which places emphasis not only on problem-solving but on the life experience provided by the program.

All levels can be concerned with normal socialization or with rehabilitation.

Information and Orientation Groups

The goal of these groups is to transmit specific information and to have members consider the implications of this information for themselves. Groups may be related, for instance, to career development, where a group comes together to consider what are the implications of selecting a particular career for them. They may be held to transmit knowledge about courses of action, as in informational groups for pregnant mothers about the course of pregnancy or hospital procedures, or to introduce clients to the workings of an agency. Attempts may also be made in these groups to introduce a new idea or refocus the contact, as to help parents see that an adolescent's problem may in reality be a family problem.

Such groups economize considerably in time. They may reduce isolation, guilt, anxiety by the recognition of a common situation. They may have value in mutual help around the use of materials. The leader in these groups is likely to take initiative and to be active. There will be a fairly high ratio of leader to member discussion and the spread of participation may not be very great. Members may be more or less active, depending on the degree to which the leader encourages their involvement. Size may vary from quite small to very large. The decision about size will depend on the number of persons who are involved and the degree to which wide participation is desired.

Discussion is likely to be fairly concrete, concerned with reality, much question and answer, with some clarification of specific situations and specific feelings about situations. Audiovisual aids and reading materials may well be used and distributed.

Although, as in all groups, there is some dynamic interaction, such as getting acquainted, setting of purpose and method of operation, and some termination maneuvers, people are not likely to become too involved and intimate with each other unless the aim is to lay the groundwork in orientation for a continuing group. Then the leader may deliberately stimulate the production of more intimate and binding discussion.

Diagnostic Groups

Orientation and information groups are very often combined with diagnostic groups in order to obtain an accurate picture of how individuals or families deal with each other. The size of the group is held to not more than 12 to 15. Much more personal material is stimulated and more dynamic interaction encouraged. However, this more intense interaction creates a problem, for very soon people begin to relate to each other more intimately, transferences are developed, and the group forms into a cohesive whole. It is necessary to ask how much pretreatment diagnosis is essential and for what purposes, and how long a group has to exist in order to obtain this data. How long can a group exist without risking disruption, separation, transfer problems, and broken contacts as a result of change? When do diagnostic groups essentially become short-term treatment?

Many clinics have started with a four-session series for diagnostic groups, only to decide that this was too long, for by the fourth session a group is well on the way to cohesion and members are developing relations and beginning to settle down, or too short because, while problems are revealed, almost nothing is settled and worked out, so that probably two sessions are adequate for diagnosis. By six sessions one has short-term problem-solving and evaluative groups.

Problem-Related Groups

Groups which are focused on specific problems or issues, whether on such matters as preparing families to become parents or helping unmarried mothers make decisions about their out-of-wedlock babies, are also normally short-term groups. The goal is to understand the ramifications of the problem, understand the alternatives for dealing with it, one's own attitudes and feelings about it, and from this to determine a course of action for its resolution. Group operations are thus limited to specific areas in the members' lives, and discussion is likely to have relevance for all.

In such groups, the leader sets the focus, then increasingly encourages members to discuss the problem themselves and to bring out their own feelings about it. He encourages self and mutual assistance. The degree to which he will encourage the group to find their own information will vary depending on the population and the setting. However, in terms of training in self-reliance, the more he can move the group to act for themselves, the more effective the group will be.

Members, through examining their problems, can begin to feel very intimate and can give each other much support; and there is generally less acting out than in less focused groups because membership is usually voluntary, interested, and concerned. Role playing can be very useful in both information and problem-related groups in teaching youth how to deal with specific situations and to gain understanding of how others may be feeling.

Because all members have a common focus and interest and can learn vicariously from each other, groups can be fairly large, up to 12 or even 15 members. Selection does not have to be rigorous. Provided all members have a common problem, the group can sustain a wide range of other differences.

Problem-related groups are generally short-term and time-limited if they are closed groups (that is, groups to which no new members are added) or else they are open-ended, with members coming and going and staying for a relatively brief period of time.

The group process in short-term closed groups is usually accelerated, and the leader needs to be aware that there will be a tendency to begin termination procedures in the last two or three sessions. In this writer's view, it is possible to discourage early and prolonged separation maneuvers without causing the final termination to be traumatic. In open-ended groups, the relationship of members to each other and to the group is likely to be less intense; and termination is on an individual basis rather than a group operation. In problem-centered open-ended groups, different facets of the problem will be brought up again and again as the needs of the attending group members vary.

Life Adjustment Groups

Such groups are concerned with the individual's way of life. They may be composed of people who are in the process of transition from one stage in their lives to another or of people who wish to make a more satisfactory adjustment and wish to learn more about themselves. The goals are to help members understand themselves, how they relate to others, what they want out of life, and how their own behavior and feelings get in their way. Goals may be merely to teach members how to work out their problems and to start a process of readjustment, or they may be to help members work through many deep-seated difficulties and to achieve a radical change in their way of life.

Although these groups are generally treatment groups, they may be conducted for people who wish to increase their own self-knowledge or their general competence, as in groups composed of group therapists in training or personal development groups in school. Methods of leading these groups vary considerably. The leader always sets the time and teaches the group how to work together. However, he may be active or passive, encourage the group members to be more or less concerned with their relationship to him or to each other. He may direct the group's attention to what is happening in the group or encourage them to bring in material from their lives outside or from their past. He may emphasize the experience or the analysis of experience. He may work in terms of any of the current theories of psychotherapy and with any of various treatment foci; on content, or the management of anxiety and defense, on member roles and group maneuvers, on underlying themes, or on transference phenomena.

Duration and intensity of treatment can vary considerably in these groups. There is no question that people differ from each other in the way they learn and the extent to which they can benefit from learning. It has also been our experience that a particular person varies from time to time in his ability to respond. Sometimes an individual is encapsulated in such a hard shell of defensiveness that only intensive and prolonged exposure will break this down sufficiently to permit change to take place. At another time, during a crisis for example, he can be so receptive that small periods of discussion can set off inner re-evaluations which will continue without further stimulation for some time. Often a single period of counseling or treatment may not be so beneficial as two periods with a break in between, during which evaluation can take place. These matters are at present subject to speculation and best judgment or mere guesswork.

Selection and grouping are also matters which require careful consideration in these groups. The more we require members to examine and possibly check the ways in which they defend themselves against intense feelings and involvement with others and set in motion the development of transference, the more carefully we must select our group members, because we need to know whether the individual is strong enough to face these revelations or whether he will be forced to increase his defenses or regress to early and more primitive ways of dealing with intolerable situations, such as a retreat from reality into psychosis.

There has recently been much experimentation with different group compositions, particularly with adolescent populations. And today we can emphasize the individual, the peer group, the family. Much of our work with younger middle-class adolescents is undertaken within a family emphasis because of the close involvement of middle-class families and the primacy of the family as a middle-class acculturation agent. With older adolescents and with lower-class teenagers in general, there is more emphasis on the individual or the peer group because the individual is already moving away from the family toward living independently.

When we are dealing with the family, we are more likely to be concerned with communication between family members, misunderstandings, mixed feelings, struggles to blackmail each other, disentanglement of individual identities and individual goals, separation of child and parent, increase of trust and autonomy, or focus on influencing the family as a group.

In the peer group, emphasis is frequently on the development of a new reference group within which we can develop a culture of mutual assistance. Members help each other examine how they deal with situations, how they appear to others. They establish a new set of standards and values and test out their sense of identity against the realities of the group.

There are some important and intrinsic differences between working with individuals, small groups of unrelated peers, a family, and several families. For example, the use of time in relation to content is different. The individual does not have to share time. The family is totally concerned with the problems of all. When several unconnected individuals or families are placed together, they must share time and attention and endure periods when the discussion has no particular relevance to themselves. In such groups, there is an exercise in learning how truly to be interested in others in altruistic fashion. In all groups, there are opportunities for identification with group members as well as the leader, while in individual treatment there is only opportunity to relate to or identify with the therapist or counselor. In the family there are limited new identifications; but in peer groups there is wide opportunity for identification; and in multiple family groups opportunity for several different kinds of identifications: with other people's fathers or mothers, with other sons or daughters, women against men, children together.

Competitive feelings are likely to be aroused in all situations, except where there is a counselor and one counselee. Competition for the leader is most intense in some individual family groups. Opportunities for reality testing are more frequent and varied in multiple family and peer groups than in individual or single family counseling. Transference is most complicated in multiple family groups, where there are parental transferences to the therapists, parent-child transferences between couples, joint parent relationships to the children, sibling transferences among all the group members in regard to the leader, libidinal relationships between couples, rivalries between families, and identifications not only as individuals but also as couples and children and as families. In individual treatment group behavior must be described, in families and group such behavior can be seen in action.

Communication is more directly influenced in family groups than in unrelated groups. Daily life is most easily influenced in task-related counseling groups. Groups of peers who also meet outside the group can put much pressure to bear on each other and can influence their neighborhood or the rest of their institution.

In totally unrelated groups, emphasis is entirely on helping the individual use the group to learn how to manage his life more satisfactorily. The more intervention is integrated with the lives of the group members, the more possible it is to emphasize and achieve change in the system of which the individual forms a part and thus primarily and secondarily to enable him to achieve change.

Indirect Counseling

Because adolescents are often particularly resistive to admitting that they have problems and already feel so insecure that it can increase their resentment and malfunctioning to concentrate on their weaknesses, efforts have been made to build both social-ization and rehabilitation into other activities; groups which are established for recreational purposes can provide many oppor-tunities for youngsters to learn how to deal with each other, increase their self-esteem, and talk over matters which bother them in their lives outside the group with sympathetic peers and group leaders. Counseling can be included as part of classroom management or job training. Focus is first on creating a positive group climate and on the strengths rather than the weaknesses of group members. Much is achieved through the relationship between group members and experiences in the group; opportunities for achievement, reality testing, and confrontation with the effects of one's behavior on others are all made easy in these groups; and problems are dealt with in a constructive way in relation to real situations. The quality of the experience is as important as any verbalization and discussion of problems.

Such groups are not usually highly selective. They may even be natural long-term groups. They may last for a short or long time. They often meet for much longer sessions than counseling or therapy groups because interpersonal growth and change is only one reason for the group to exist, and formal learning content or fun will also take up much time.

Regression is kept to a minimum in these groups. There is no encouragement of fantasy or unconscious thoughts; the work of the group is concerned with ego development and with reality, on such matters as how people see themselves, how others feel about them, what they can do, what they want to do, what they believe in, and how they manage different situations.

Leader's Attitude toward the Group and Its Members

A paradox of all intervention is that while a leader can be considered competent only if he is helpful to those with whom he works, he must not be so invested in the group members that a change in any one of them in a certain direction becomes the measure of his competence and self-respect. That is to say, pupils, patients, and clients must be respected as individuals who have autonomy over their own lives and who have a right to choose how they will lead those lives. The task of the leader is to establish an appropriate group climate within which he can enable those with whom he works to understand their situations, feelings, and needs as adequately as possible and make and carry out choices and decisions with full understanding of the implications of their actions.

Undoubtedly, any group leader, and particularly one who works with children and adolescents, represents certain standards and values and presents himself as a model for identification. When he is leading a group, he attempts to teach the group these standards so that they may exert an influence on each other.

Teaching their young how to live within the range of acceptable behavior and to accept their standards and values is the task of all viable societies; and society rewards those who conform, penalizes most of those who do not comply, and permits a few mavericks to live deviant lives in view of their special value to the society. In order to obtain compliance, the connection between conformity and the rewards, as well as the penalties, has to be made clear. In modern metropolitan society, for many there has been a disconnection between the rewards and the conformity, so that deviant and delinquent groups have developed which have set up their own standards of operation and their own rewards for behavior which is inimical to and in defiance of society.

However, even if the rewards for behavior are clearly seen, often such behavior will still be rejected by many if conformity threatens the autonomy of the individual, if he does not have real confidence he can succeed, or if he has to sacrifice too much security to obtain the reward.

The leader is critical to the group. Through his selection of members and his direction, he will establish the climate of the group and influence how it will operate. A leader teaches a group how to function 1) by definite statements about how to operate, limits, and so on, as at the beginning of a group; 2) by his own activities, such as asking questions, focusing on certain levels of exploration; 3) by selective attention, that is, what he focuses on, what he ignores; 4) by his own attitudes expressed verbally or nonverbally; 5) by statements about standards and values.

The group leader plays many roles. He is a teacher, a reflector, an informant and resource man, an explorer, a model for identification, a clarifier, an interpreter, a transmitter of values, a supporter (someone who cares and respects the group members). In his work he can choose to emphasize one or more of these roles; what he chooses and what levels he works at will depend very much on the population and on the goals of the group. A leader must know his population, understand the significance of behavior, and be able to communicate in their language.

The Use of Authority in Treatment

Essentially it must be recognized that no fundamental personality change or alterations in value systems or ways of life can be achieved except by the individual concerned, so that authority can be used only (1) to expose individuals to the opportunity to change; (2) to increase motivation for change. Ultimately, the individual must invest himself in the treatment, or no change will take place.

Authority may be used to force members to attend a group where the leader himself has no authority. A group may be set up so that the leader is an independent and outside person subject to the rules of the particular setting only in regard to attendance and if behavior extends beyond the room. In general, all that goes on within the room is confidential within very broad limits; and members may do things within the room which are not permitted outside. The leader has no ordinary obligation to report transgressions unless they appear really dangerous to the individual and the community, but rather to help the members analyze the consequences and take responsibility. The group leader generally plays a benevolent, trusted, neutral, and permissive role.

The leader may have authority in other areas but take no power in the group. The leader may be a person such as a guidance counselor or welfare officer who leads a group for certain purposes, in which he has no authority or abdicates authority. However, he has certain kinds of responsibility—if information is told him in these areas, he has responsibility to investigate it outside the group.

Authority may be vested in the leader of the group so that he can affect the members lives. The leader may have power over his group members. Performance in the group may affect privileges the members may obtain. The leader or the group may be able to apply sanctions.

In probation groups, the leader or the group may decide whether an individual should be returned to court for violation of probation. A guidance counselor may have to decide or have the group decide what should be done about a member who is playing hooky. Performance in the group may be the deciding factor as to when an individual is permitted to leave the hospital.

The degree to which the leader delegates this decision-making power to the group affects his role and position in the group. A leader who makes decisions does not encourage his members to take responsibility for themselves. He increases their dependence on him. A leader has to make clear, however, if he delegates decision-making to the group, the limits of the power which he is willing to give up and the limits of his own mandate of power vis-à-vis the institution.

Confidentiality

The definition of confidentiality has two main parts. Confidentiality of group or individual sessions implies that (1) the therapist or group leader will not reveal what he has learned in the session to anyone outside the session; (2) that members will not reveal to others what has gone on in the sessions. Related to these is the legal issue of privileged communication, which will be discussed elsewhere.

Obviously, agreement about confidentiality is part of the ground rules; and equally obviously, there are degrees of confidentiality which can be established between members and leaders. First, in traditional casework and psychotherapy the most usual agreement has been that the leader would not discuss any materials learned in the group with anyone other than agency professionals engaged in assisting him without prior consent of the individual concerned. This worked relatively smoothly with adult neurotic patients who came for help because they were very uncomfortable and wished relief. However, it becomes a different problem when one is working with adolescents and their parents or with character problems where the individual is accepting counseling more or less because of external pressure. Group leaders are frequently caught in situations where parent and adolescent each reveals confidentially to their own leader, or even the same leader, material which it would be extremely useful to discuss with the other but which they do not release. Both talk about matters in their daily lives which need to be dealt with, but give no permission to do so. It is wise for the leader to make clear initially that family members will be expected to work out problems together and that the leader may call the family together if such problems have to be resolved. Delinquents in and out of institutions can trap the leader (as in a group where the leader had promised to keep everything secret and was then told by one of the members that he had stolen the keys of the institution), or they can raise his anxiety by telling of crimes committed or about to be committed, involvement with drug taking or other serious crises, and at the same time witholding permission for anyone to take action. The leader is then caught in his own promises. He is faced with the alternatives of standing by without intervening and watching disaster occur or intervening and losing the trust of the youngster. This dilemma is one which certain kinds of neurotic and psychopathic patients try to set up for their own destruction. They prove at any cost that no one can be relied upon and relieve themselves of responsibility for their own fate. While it might be argued that the nonacceptance of this responsibility by the leader is an important part of treatment, operationally, it is preferable to be left free to maneuver without the complication of a clear betrayal of trust. The obvious necessity is to understand the maneuver and to help the youngster understand the way in which he sabotages himself. Unless ground rules are made clear, individuals, families, and groups can become caught in the use of confidentiality as a resistance to change and the resolution of problems.

Closely allied to this problem, and often confused with it, is the leader's right to bring into the group or face the individual or group members with actions and information culled from persons outside the group. This has essentially nothing to do with confidentiality, but with the concept of the leader as a neutral person outside and detached from the individual's life, with no direct influence or responsibility over it and consequently to be confided in without any possibility of sanctions. This concept may or may not be useful. With motivated neurotics, the patients themselves want to help at a conscious level and consequently are mostly willing and strong enough to bring their problems for discussion. When dealing with persons who characteristically deny and avoid facing problems and do not take such responsibility, this procedure does not work; and the leader's task is to move the individual to the place where he can and will take such responsibility for himself.

Second, while it is important that group members feel free to discuss any part of their lives with each other and learn to trust and help each other, it is important to set up a code so that people do not gossip about each other's business outside the group.

In groups where members have contact with each other in their daily lives, such as in school, institutional, or training groups, and where mutual help is considered central to the operations of the group, members are expected to bring up each other's problems in the group if they know about them. This goes counter to self-protective, anti-authoritarian systems such as child-adult or delinquent systems in which lower echelons classically band together against the power structure and in which the squealer betrays his fellows. For group members to be able to help each other, they must feel that there is a unity of purpose between staff and group members which can eliminate the antagonism and the dichotomy. Even though such freedom is encouraged within the group, it may well be that care must be taken that members do not use such information as weapons against each other outside.

Selection

If one reads the literature, one will find many discussions of how to select members for counseling and therapy groups. Questions are raised whether one should have unisexual or heterosexual groups, groups of patients with one symptom or many, groups composed of members who behave in the same or in different ways. Frequently, however, there is little discussion of several prior questions: Why we select; whether we should select; and if selection is appropriate, who should make the selection, the group members or the leader.

It is important to recognize that there are two orders of selection. First, the selection of members who are suitable for a particular kind of group program, and second, the grouping of members in a group.

Why do we select at all? What are the purposes of selection and grouping? First, to get the individuals to come to a particular kind of group because we know it is designed to meet their needs. Sometimes we merely describe a service and let people select themselves. However, it is always important that the group will be appropriate and relevant to the goals of the individual. Second, selection is made in an attempt to screen out people who will not benefit from the service. Third, it is designed to economize by putting together people with similar needs. Fourth, we select in order to create a particular kind of group.

We sort people into different groups to provide particular interactions which we assume will be beneficial; to develop a specific climate and to promote control of the group through the interaction of the members with each other; and to avoid placing people together who will have a detrimental effect on each other. For instance, too many teenagers who are all hostile and anti-authoritarian will make a group very difficult to lead and may result in a reinforcement of anti-social attitudes. Too many depressed, passive youngsters may cause the leader to do all the work. The degree to which we have to take grouping into consideration will depend largely on our group management. A highly structured group is much less dependent on its membership than one in which little direction comes from the leader.

Our selection criteria inevitably will have to be related to our goals, and depending on these there will be a big difference in how much we need to know about individual group members. If we are setting up a short-term counseling series, "How one goes about choosing a career and looking for a job," we may decide to open it to all people who are interested in this subject or to all junior high school or high school students. We may, however, be particularly concerned with a certain class of student who is selecting a career and whom we want to assist in this search for appropriate work, so that already we become more selective. We may become even more selective and decide we are interested only in a particular group, such as delinquents or retardates who are unable to live in the community and who need help in finding and preparing for a foster home or residence, or for sheltered work.

In grouping, we must consider the degree to which difference can be tolerated in any group. If adolescents are working on general life adjustment and reviewing their values, they will find it much harder to work together if they are drawn from very different backgrounds. However, if they are focusing on solving a commonly held problem, their backgrounds and general life situations may be irrelevant and much more difference can be accepted.

In a group of teen-agers who are struggling with how to manage their lives, we shall be concerned with developmental levels, age and high school grade, life style and social class, for teenage values and ways of behaving vary greatly from one grade to another and between older and younger boys and girls. However, in a group of unmarried mothers who are trying to make a decision about the disposition of their babies, we shall not be concerned with these factors. We shall use the problem of unmarried motherhood as the central focus so that all will feel mutual identification, and the discussion will be relevant to everyone.

Whether we include both boys and girls in a program or only one sex will depend on the purposes of the groups and the age of the youngsters. If we are discussing a particular problem such as diabetes, there seems to be no reason why both sexes should not be included. Young teen-agers, on the other hand, are usually freer to discuss many of their personal difficulties without the presence of the other sex. Older adolescents can often benefit from an understanding of the point of view of the opposite sex. In heterosexual grouping, developmental material as well as chronological age should be considered. Girls of 15 are quite frequently interested in boys; but many boys of 15 are still concerned only with school, sports, and other boys. Ages and grades have many feelings attached to them. If a group member has to admit he is older than others, yet he is in a junior class, he may well feel placed in an inferior position, an important fact to take into consideration in grouping.

Individuals who may appropriately be treated in one kind of group may not fit into another. A very poorly controlled schizophrenic boy may do well in a highly structured, relatively unstimulating group, whereas he may fall to pieces in an unstructured and permissive activity group.

Preparation

For problem-centered and unindividualized programs and for orientation or diagnostic groups, we may merely invite people to attend or ask agencies to refer members who have specific, defined characteristics. If we are concerned with setting up groups where the composition of the group itself in regard to the characteristics of the individuals is important, then much more data has to be obtained; and it may be very desirable for the leader to interview each candidate personally.

Where the purposes of the group are clear and uncontroversial and there is no need for highly individualized goals, members can be invited or referred without any special preparation. If, however, the reasons for becoming a member of a group need clarification or refocusing or if there is a question of motivation, then a decision has to be made whether individuals should be contacted prior to the group either by the leader or by some other agency or referral staff members, or whether an orientation group should be held for these purposes.

However preparation for the group is undertaken, the purposes of the group must seem relevant to the candidate. For example, if a teen-ager denies that he is in difficulty, it is unlikely that he will accept a general invitation to come to a treatment group. A decision has to be made whether resistance and defense can be and have to be worked out through individual contact or whether it may be possible to include the teen-ager in some other kind of group, such as a recreational club or a career preparation group into which counseling is built. Sometimes youngsters have had such bad experiences with adults that no initial one-to-one contact is productive. On the other hand, there are boys and girls who are so fearful of being part of a group that they must first become comfortable with the group leader alone.

Even if a group program is planned for normal teen-agers as part of the normal socialization process, prospective members must know why the group is being established, what its purposes are, how it will be conducted, who will be the leader, what the group will demand of the members, where it will take place, under what auspices, at what times, and what the ground rules will be. They should be encouraged to reflect on why they should be included and to formulate what they expect to obtain from the experience.

Interpretation of the group should always be in terms of its particular focus and, if to an individual, in terms of that particular individual's needs. In our society it has been customary to consider personal problems as private matters. A youngster may well quite appropriately question why he might be required to talk in a group with a lot of strangers about the trouble he is having making friends. It can be pointed out that it is in just such a group that he can begin to learn why he has these difficulties, for, as the group forms and he and the other members get to know each other, he will demonstrate his particular patterns of relating to others and members can share with him their reactions.

Frequently in preparing teen-agers and their families for treatment groups, it is necessary to refocus the problem. Parents bring their adolescents to clinics and complain about their children's difficulties or bad behavior. The adolescent is often very angry at being made the focus of the family difficulty. He may even feel that it is his parents' problem. He may be right, for quite often trouble with the children obscures basic difficulties between couples. At some point these problems have to be restated more in keeping with reality. It is often very useful to discuss with all the family initially what seems to be a family problem in which all are involved.

Group Size

The size of the group will be determined by its purpose. If a group is assembled so that information can be disseminated and little personal discussion is expected or few relations solicited, the group can be large. If everyone is expected to take part, it is usually hard to manage a group of more than 12 people. When close relationships and a cohesive group are desired, it may be preferable to reduce the numbers to 8 or 10 members. If it is planned to discuss very intimate material, an even smaller group of 4 to 6 members may be preferable.

A second factor which needs to be taken into consideration in deciding upon the size of the group is the nature of the members. Members who are very reticent and shy or members who wander off into daydreams are more easily involved if groups are kept small. If members do not attend regularly or are poorly motivated, then it is wise to add some extra members. If members find it hard to be interested in other people, then a small group is preferable. On the other hand, where all have a common problem a large group is productive. For example, in a group of unmarried mothers where the situation and decisions were common to all, not all girls wanted to talk. They felt they learned a great deal from listening to others who wanted actively to present their problems. Thus, a large group of 12 to 16 girls was manageable. A discussion of the implications of giving up the baby was very moving to all, even though only 4 out of a group of 12 took part, because the topic had significance for everybody in the group. But when members are really examining their own particular situation and trying to understand how they feel and what they are doing, groups should be small, even though other members may have similar, general problems. When one girl states in a group that someone has molested her, even though all girls may have fantasies and anxieties about rape, there are very special elements in this particular situation which have to be explored. The group should be small enough so that those concerned can take an active part in the discussion. If a group is focused on the behavior manifested in the group, then everyone has to have a chance to examine his behavior.

Duration of the Group

Groups vary in the length of time which they will last. They may assemble for one session, as in many diagnostic or information groups. They may be time-limited, or they may last for several years. Other things being equal, the shorter the group the less radical the change likely to be expected, although this may not be true during periods of crisis or if one can stimulate an intense situation.

Groups can also be carried on for the same aggregate of time but spread over a longer or shorter period. Although certain differences have been hypothesized, no one at this time knows the difference in effect between groups held for intensive periods, such as all day, weekend, or weekly workshops, as against sessions held once a week or twice a week over several months or years.

It is assumed that intimacy is more easily achieved when meetings are held more frequently and that greater emotional intensity can thus be stimulated. Defenses are less likely to be reinstated when sessions follow each other rapidly. However, space between meetings often gives time for individuals to think independently and to work out their own difficulties and to realize their doubts or anxieties. It also stimulates less dependency and may encourage more self-responsibility.

The Setting

When we consider where the group program will be lodged, we need to consider the image of the institution within the community, the function of the institution, its organization, its resources, and its physical attributes.

As we have noted, an institution may be connected in the minds of parents and teen-agers with certain functions, good or bad. It may be a place where pleasurable or disagreeable happenings have already been experienced. The institution may be connected with particular populations, racial, cultural, or class, and others may feel reluctant to go there. An institution may be considered of high or low status. Drop-outs may feel very differently about attending a training program at a university than they would attending the same program housed in a school. A counseling group entitled "How teen-agers manage their parents" and housed in a recreation center may attract many boys and girls who would not agree to go to essentially the same group held in a psychiatric clinic and interpreted to them as an opportunity for teen-agers who are having difficulty with their parents to work out their problems. Clinics are for the "crazy," and problems mean inadequacy. Teen-agers are particularly sensitive to these implications. However, it must be noted that success breeds success. If a first group in a clinic goes well and members benefit, both authorities and teen-agers are more likely to support next efforts. If a girl becomes more attractive, happier, or more popular through a group program, other girls who would like to succeed may refer themselves.

When a program is housed within an institution it must be fully accepted by that institution and complement its function. As McCorkle, et al.[1] found out when they attempted to run a permissive group in an authoritarian and punitive institution, all kinds of difficulties are created and the program can well be sabotaged. Essentially, any group program should be integrated in its milieu, and all parts of an institution should reinforce each other. Group goals should be congruent with the defined goals of the institution.

It goes without saying that the administrators of an agency must accept, want, and understand the group program. It is important also that all who deal with teen-agers understand and accept the program and have considered how their roles relate to it. If a group is led in a school, the teachers, principal, assistant principal, counselors, school nurse, school psychologist, students, and parents all have to reach some agreement about its purposes, how it should be conducted, how their roles interrelate, how they will communicate, and how they will handle crises. If power struggles develop among the staff, this trouble will be reflected in the group. If staff who are referring or preparing youngsters for the group do not understand the program, it is hard for them to be convinced of its value and to prepare candidates effectively.

The rules under which the group will operate have to be worked out. Who sets the limits? If adolescents leave their group room and start running all over the building, is this all right? If not, who stops them and who is held responsible? These arrangements will vary with the purpose of the group and the method through which it is conducted. Who will handle non-attendance at groups? If there is trouble in other parts of the teen-agers'

[1] McCorkle et al., *The Highfields Story.*

lives, should this be reported to the group leader or left to the individual to bring up?

Procedures for communication have to be established. What kind of information and records does the group leader need? What does the institution need? How will contact be maintained between staff and other services?

It is essential that someone be made administratively responsible for the group program who has sufficient interest and power to see that its needs are taken care of. Membership has to be maintained, space reserved, supplies obtained if necessary. Timing is often important in setting up groups, and a program can fail to get off the ground because of poor organization.

Decisions about the nature of the group will also be affected by the qualifications of the staff and the availability of supervisors. These will be considered in more detail under the appropriate sections of this book.

The physical attributes of any institution must be considered. For discussion groups, a room has to be available which will contain the requisite number of members and which can be reserved regularly and without interruption. It is very destructive to a group to have people walk in and out, for privacy is usually important. If the group has to be moved because the room is requested for other purposes, this gives the impression that it is not valued; and the teen-agers feel they are being treated like second-class citizens, a point on which they are usually very sensitive.

The atmosphere of a group can be affected by the size, shape, and color of a room. One which is long and narrow tends to have a sobering effect on the group and to limit participation because of the way in which members are seated. It has been demonstrated experimentally that participation is facilitated and spread more widely when members are seated in a circle and that the distance between members influences the type of communication. Hall has demonstrated that in every culture the distance between persons who are conversing intimately is much less than when they are transacting business. Spatial distance, size of group, and quality of discussion are all closely related.

The kinds of seats which are provided will also influence the group. Sitting around a table tends to be more business-like and less relaxed than lounging in comfortable chairs. Whether there is a specific place for the leader, such as the head of the table or a different kind of chair, has implications for the conduct of the group. Such an arrangement lends itself to a more directive approach. In a permissive group, the leader may choose to vary where he sits or even to move slightly out of the circle.

If activities are planned, adequate space must be provided and supplies available. Too small a room builds up pressure. A very large space allows for evasion and adds to feelings of diffusion and anxiety.

Program Coordination

A major problem in modern metropolitan society is the coordination of different programs. Attention needs to be addressed to the development of overall community standards and expectations; to the meshing of education and career planning; to the provision of cultural and recreational experiences which will enhance and buttress the adolescent's life and provide opportunities for initiative and emotional satisfaction and outlets for the teen-ager's energy.

Summary

In setting up a group program, the following factors have to be taken into consideration:

1. The needs of the population must be identified and purposes, methods, and goals clearly defined.

2. There must be an adequate number of adolescents who require the same form of treatment. Members must be selected and grouped appropriately in terms of the group and the level of operation.

3. The duration of the group should be related to its purpose.

4. An adequately trained leader must be available or a leader who has some potential for and interest in leading groups and who can obtain supervision or consultation.

5. The program must be interpreted to all concerned and individual resistances among the staff worked out.

6. It has to be recognized that the setting of the group and the relationships existing between group, institution, and community will set the limits and influence what kind of group can be run.

7. All persons concerned with the group and its members need to be clear as to their respective roles.

8. The limits of confidentiality should be clearly recognized by all.

9. Someone must be administratively responsible so that the program runs smoothly. Proper preparation and timing are important factors in running groups.

10. Methods for the effective evaluation of the group and for program control should be worked out and established.

11. Integration between services and integrated program planning for individuals are very important aspects of any intervention with adolescents. As far as possible, problems should be treated within the normal institutions and should use strengths and tasks rather than difficulties and weaknesses as the focus. Integration between groups also includes regular feedback and close collaboration so that problems can be identified and worked on as soon as they arise.

V

Process and Maneuvers in Adolescent Groups

In all groups there is a certain progression whether the group lasts for an hour or several years. Somehow the members must become acquainted, establish a common purpose, decide how they are going to operate, conduct their business, and eventually disband. However, in any group which is going to continue over a span of time, much more has to occur. Relationships develop between members. Members combine and compete for leadership and position. Emotional demands will be made on the group, the members, and the leader. Members will learn to trust and care for each other. They will come to have meaning for each other. New standards and ways of behaving will be created and upheld by the group. A continuous dynamic interaction will take place.

The Beginning

Whether their group is a counseling, psychotherapeutic, training, or recreational group, members initially expect that the leader will structure the group and will tell them how to operate. If he does not do this, the group becomes anxious and often resentful. Members will begin to pressure the leader to undertake this task. Adolescents, even though they wish to be independent, are no exception and do not like the suggestion that the group is to function as they see fit, although if the leader does structure the group they may be quite apt to oppose his suggestions. The more the leader defines the structure of the group, the more responsibility he takes for its operation, the more he fosters dependency. In a recreational group for young boys strictly programmed by the leader, the members did not learn how to plan for themselves, although they met weekly for a year. With a new leader, who gave the boys freedom to plan, they were able to take full responsibility after a very short period of confusion. Most groups (even consisting of psychologically handicapped members), if left with a free hand, will learn to make some plans in relatively few sessions. Adults are all too prone to feel youngsters are "not ready," to keep members dependent, and thus to prevent them from growing and developing.

From the start, group members struggle to become acquainted with each other. Mutual introductions are usually a formality, and names are not absorbed at the first go around. Members gradually ask each other increasingly intimate questions. However, most groups hesitate for some time on the edge of self-revelation. If formal roles are not established, members feel out each other's strengths and weaknesses and test the strength of the leader.

Testing Operations

The beginnings of these groups are typically concerned with mutual identification, the question of trust, the ambivalence about revealing and admitting to any problems, and the anxiety about being crazy. The members test the therapist and the group. They are concerned with the following issues:

1. What will the leader and the group think of me? How do I rate? Will they like me?
2. What are the other members like? Can I like and trust them?
3. Is the leader competent? Can I trust him? Is he dependable? What will he permit?

4. What kind of group is this? Is it a good group? Can I get what I need in this group?
5. What do the other members want to do in this group?

In the ongoing conduct of the group, the leader needs to be clear about his values and the limits of what he will tolerate in the group, for the members need the reassurance that they will not be permitted to disrupt the group completely. This is in contrast to the latency group, where on the whole the ego is more stable, and there is less likelihood of impulsivity getting out of control. Emotional contagion is an important factor in this period. This does not mean that the leader should start off the group with a number of prohibitions delineating the limits, but rather that he should be personally secure in what he will and will not tolerate.

Adolescents do not want to be able to overcome and defeat the leader, but they will try because they need to know whether they can trust and rely on him in their struggle for self-sufficiency. They will secretly hope that he can maintain control, for if they can defeat him then he is seen to be weak and can be of no use to them.

Testing operations in adolescent groups include some or all of the following: griping against authority; complaining and blaming others; attacking the leader verbally, directly or indirectly; seeing whether he will permit things which they know are not allowable; trying to use him as a tool against other authority; trying to make him angry; seducing him into delinquent acts; trying to make him disapprove; proving that they cannot trust him; trying to get him into a power struggle where they can defeat him; seeing whether he will betray them; scapegoating and attacking others, seeing if they can drive a member out of the group; testing whether the leader will play favorites or be pushed into defending and protecting the weaker members, thus emphasizing their weaknesses and infantilizing them.

Absences and Lateness

Absences and lateness can be manifestations of individual or group resistances but in either case are disturbing to the group. The members should be encouraged to examine these behaviors as an offense against them, preventing them from getting the most out of their group sessions, and a tradition should be established from the beginning that all such problems will be taken up in the group. However, if a member is absent because he is particularly anxious or upset, it may be that the leader will have to get in touch with him and talk over his situation first outside the group.

During the beginning phase, when the group is developing an identity, members are often very concerned about whether they are going to form a worthwhile group. They are afraid to lose any members, as if they felt that if one goes the whole may fly apart. Any differences or disagreements between members make everyone anxious. The following is an example of a group session after a member has threatened to leave:

C: Well, what's he trying to prove by saying he's not coming back?

G: Did he express why he wasn't coming back?

B: Well, why do we have to get off on him again? Why don't we talk about who is angry? We're angry right now.

F: I'm angry, and I'm angry at A. because he's not coming back.

C: That's right. I am too.

F: Because for him not coming back and taking that attitude . . .

G: (interrupting F) The whole group falls apart . . .

F: The whole group is lost . . .

G: . . . when one person stops.

C: The minute we say anything at all.

F: That's what I was told when I wanted to drop out of the group. If one quits and another one can quit, and another can quit . . .

D: . . . if this is to go on week after week and I know if A. comes back everyone is going to sit here afraid to say anything.

P: I think it should be settled with A. sitting here.

DR. T: Why are you afraid of saying things? What is this feeling that if he drops out the whole group disintegrates?

F: Well . . . if he drops out, if it happens to him and it hurts him, so next week we'll say, poor J. sittin' over there and there was something, we were irritated about what he said, so we jumped him and the first thing he goes home.

F: . . . then you have no group, so why the hell did I come here for—I just wasted all this time.

DR. T: No one has said that. In fact, you know the group will not fall apart. A member comes to get help. It is the responsibility of others to help him face his difficulties, even if he finds this hard and sometimes painful.

Facing Differences

As the group becomes more cohesive, members feel more secure with each other so that differences are more easily faced and anger with each other can be expressed. If members who have been ill-treated by the group threaten to leave, the group may become very anxious and guilty. Unless the leader intervenes, it may inhibit their capacity to face differences, to express feelings, and to disagree. When such a climate prevails, it is not possible to work out problems.

It seems important, in whatever kind of group is conducted with adolescents, that an undefensive posture is fostered. The group members need to recognize that difficulties and differences are natural and that they should be concerned for each other and willing to stay with problems and to work them out.

In fostering this attitude, the group leader must be able to look at and discuss his own behavior without having to insist that he is always right. If an adolescent complains that the leader didn't help enough, did not tell him what to do or stop him from making a mistake, it may be an excellent idea to examine what went into the leader's decision, what his posture was, and whether he took the appropriate attitude or not. If the leader does not have to be perfect, the group members can also err; and this makes it much easier for all to face their mistakes.

There can be disagreements between members and leader about what is an appropriate reaction. The leader may have one purpose in this, and the group member may want something else. A member may desire to have his dependency needs satisfied, whereas the leader may be concerned with having him recognize the reality of his own strength in facing difficulty. The leader must be able to accept this difference and make clear his own position.

A boy who had always been over-protected by his mother provoked another boy into a fight. He then called out to the leader, "Help me, help me!" The leader paid no attention, and the fight finished quickly with the provoker receiving a punch on the nose. The boy turned on the leader in a rage. "Why didn't you help me? I called to you." The leader replied calmly, "I didn't think you needed any help. You are big enough to take care of yourself." Group work is not manipulation. It must always foster self-determination.

Competition

Competition goes on constantly in groups. Competition with the leader and for the leader; for the attention, control and/or approval of the group. Each member of the group is secretly busy comparing himself with all other group members. Subtly or openly, the youngsters work to try to establish a pecking order, although in a dynamic group in which members are growing this never becomes static. Some vie openly for leadership in the group. Others sit back and assess the situation. Still others move into accustomed roles of the sick or weak or isolate, for group members unconsciously set up for themselves the roles they are accustomed to playing and use the kind of defenses and resistances they normally use.

Some people compete in groups by working very hard on their problems, by being good, by currying favor with the leader. Other people compete with attention-getting, disruptive, boasting behavior; others by being plaintive, by being stupid. Members use the same methods and play the same roles as in their own families.

In some families the only way to get attention from parents is to cause trouble. Trouble is rewarded with attention even if it has to be paid for. Similarly with stupidity: some children get no reward for success; but although approval is unobtainable, they can get attention if they fail. These patterns are repeated in the group. In one group, one of the girls who felt she was stupid would begin to act up and create a physical disturbance or talk about some meaningless piece of gossip whenever any of the others reported any success in school. The competition for attention and the different ways they tried to obtain it was discussed with the girls; and their mutual feelings of worthlessness and inability to feel loved and accepted for themselves alone were revealed, after which the need to be so disruptive died away.

Member Roles

Some youngsters if they do not get attention give up and will not join. They have to be the favorite or nothing. They will avoid coming or stay on the edge of the group. It is very useful to know the customary roles of group members and their methods

of getting attention before they come into the group. This behavior is often considered in individual treatment primarily as a
means of handling anxiety; however, in a group its obvious role
function becomes clearly visible and can be usefully discussed.

Group members can play many different roles; the co-leader,
the asker of questions, the finder of quick solutions, the con-
soler, the conscience, the good child, the coherer, the manipu-
lator, the conformist, the one who is weak, sick, or special, the
one who is silent, stupid, or victimized, the one who blames
others, the superior one.[1]

In any counseling or therapy group, members and leader find
it hard to tolerate a member who consistently denies any difficulty and assumes a position of superiority to others. One must
recognize that such members are usually very insecure. They
need to prove themselves and also to keep from exposing themselves. It is also usually true that such attitudes give the individual trouble outside the group as well. Such individuals need support in feeling more secure. Once they feel less anxious they will
have less need to be perfect. The leader must understand the
problem so that he does not get annoyed, for while it is fine to
have heated discussions and for members to confront each
other, it is important not to encourage the group to attack each
other in a destructive way.

People who insist on finding immediate surface solutions and
who give endless advice may be popular at first, but after a time
they begin to annoy the group because they cut off feelings and
discussion. It is sometimes possible to point out to such people
that the members are not yet ready to find a solution, but are
interested first in examining what is involved in a situation.
Sometimes it may be important to inquire why they need an answer so fast. For many people, ambiguity and lack of clear direction are hard to tolerate.

The defenses people adopt in groups are usually not only

1 Powdermaker and Frank, *Group Psychology: Studies in Methodology*.

ways in which they deal with their anxiety, but also have significance for the way they perceive themselves and the way in which they have attained satisfaction in the past. All defensive operations carry satisfactions as well as limitations. A boy who was having difficulty in performing in school, although he was very intelligent, continually acted stupid in the group. His comments always seemed off the point. The group members began to get irritated. Some attacked him while others were supportive, so that he became the focus of attention. The leader raised the question why he was always missing the point, although he was bright, and asked what advantages this operation carried for him. It was finally revealed that he had not been able to compete in his family with his father and elder brother, both very aggressive people, but that he received attention and protection from his mother through acting weak and stupid. In the family as in the group, he had divided the members and focused a conflict around him, thus gaining attention even at the price of failure. Once he was able to recognize this maneuver, he was able to give up acting stupid and mobilize himself to learn and succeed.

Individual Resistances

In both counseling and therapy groups, members individually or as a group avoid involvement in task-related discussion by means of a number of different operations known as resistances. Individual members resist through silence; inconsequential chatter; avoiding important issues; diverting discussion from important issues; obsessing, that is, repeating issues which could be important, but which are not dealt with; refusing to take responsibility; complaining; fighting; not coming; monopolizing; vacillating; listing, that is, elaborating on categories and classes of people, things, or events, without relevance to the problem or to their meaning; demanding help; asking others to make decisions; focusing on the problems of others and taking the role of helper consistently; boasting; withholding data; questioning without analyzing and following through to a solution; agreeing, complying; intellectualizing.

Collaborative Resistance

Members combine with others in resistance through mutual support; mutual admiration; fighting; joining in diversionary tactics, physical or verbal; moving away from important issues or bringing up irrelevancies, sliding off the point; competing with others; scapegoating; setting up cliques; engaging in splinter group activities; playing secrets; discussing important material outside, but not in a group; allowing members to monopolize the group's attention; mutual transference; group silence; uniting against the leader in opposition or in disruptive behavior; combining to intellectualize or argue; discussing absent members; absenteeism; lateness.

Arguing as a Defense

The following is a group discussion using arguing as a defense against dealing with real issues:

LEADER: I am not asking who started or any right and wrong in it. All I am asking is, do you know what put you in the argument and why?

C: If you start arguing, you know why.

D: I think if you see a misunderstanding between two girls, if you want to find out something about it, you let it go on for a while, let it drop for a while, take ten minutes and start on it again. Let it drop. We are here to get something settled. Not to be arguing.

A: When we start arguing, I think you should tell us to take a break.

R: I think when an argument starts, I think you should try to find out whether everybody is just trying to defend themselves, who's right and who's wrong. Nobody is going to say they are wrong.

A: I thought when we came in you would tell us what happened, you would be able to improve the thing. You look like you are going to do something else.

LEADER: I think we need to try and find out why we get into these arguments, and what we are really defending.

In this excerpt, the members also attempt to shift responsibility for their self-management onto the leader, an example of Bion's "dependency demand."

All of these resistances are important for the leader, whether they be individual or group centered. How such actions are dealt with by the leader will determine the direction and movement of the group. When the leader fails to help the group deal with resistance by individuals, the purposefulness of the group is reduced.

Monopolization

In many of these operations, the group as a whole permits and uses the individual's resistances in its own desire to avoid dealing with the tasks at hand and to avoid change. Monopolization is an interesting example. Frequently a group leader is plagued by an individual member who constantly takes over the discussion and holds the floor so that no one else can express an opinion. Why does an individual behave in this way? There can be a number of reasons. He may have a strong need to obtain the attention of the group at any cost. He may be preoccupied with himself and his own problems and unable to take any interest in others. He may be unable to tolerate silence and so anxious that he has to talk if no one else moves in fast. He may use talking as a means to avoid dealing with disturbing subjects. He may be unable through anxiety to stop talking and to let go of a subject once he gets started. He may need to reassure himself about his status by proving to the group that he is knowledgeable.

A group does not have to permit such monopolization. There can, however, be many reasons why they go along with it. First, they may feel that the monopolizer really needs attention and support, and they remain silent out of concern for him. They may also identify strongly with his need to talk and feel that to break in would be considered a very hurtful and hostile act. Often patients who have difficulty starting to talk themselves have this attitude. It sometimes happens that the monopolizers make other members so angry that they are afraid to deal with him for fear of attacking him too severely. They may also welcome the fact that they are relieved of responsibility to talk and to face their problems. They may sense that monopolization annoys the group leader and support it as a means of attacking and defeating him. The monopolizer may amuse the group and genuinely divert it from the true purpose of the meeting. Sometimes the monopolizer is actually the spokesman for the group, and what he is saying is supported by all.

The leader in dealing with the problem has to understand the motives of the individual and the position of the group. He has several choices. He can allow the monopolization to continue in the expectation that the group members will eventually become so bored and restless that they will deal with it. He can ask the group why they are allowing an individual to do all the talking. He can raise a similar question with the individual. He can be more directive in suggesting that others might participate. He can direct questions to others, demonstrating a need for wider participation; or he can analyze the situation as he sees it. In making his decision, he will take into consideration not only the positions of the individuals and the group but also the level and the goals of the group operations and the developmental status of the group.

Avoidance

Groups sometimes want to talk about a problem which has great significance for them but at the same time are anxious about tackling it. They will use a variety of diversionary tactics, and the leader must help them face what they really want to talk about. The following example begins with M. saying her father was in the hospital for a leg injury. The leader asks questions about her father's condition, but there is no response. The girls are busy exchanging nuts and gum. When there is relative quiet, D. says that she wants to talk, then doesn't have a thing to say, will keep it to herself.

L: What is she going to keep to herself?
D: What I've got on my mind.

L. persists in asking what she has on her mind. The leader wonders whether D. can talk about why she can't talk.

D: I'm going to get the hospital report today.

M. tells the group about her report card, and there is some talk about school. The leader asks why no one responds to D.'s remark. L. says she told her father she was going to be a "Dog psychiatrist" to take care of him. There is general laughter. The leader again points out that they are not responding to D. The girls seem to be listening.

D: Last Thursday I got the shock of my life.

L. asks if this is what D. was talking about before the group meeting. J. says to let L. tell it. L. looks the other way. J. tells L. to tell it. D. demands attention.

D: Now do you want to hear? I can't start.
L: Okay, I'll say it.

D. doesn't give her a chance but tells the group what is on her mind.

Adolescents are keenly adept at forcing adults into decision-making roles. The leader has to be on guard against taking responsibility which belongs to the group. This is particularly true in the formative group sessions where boys and girls are seeking out the limits of what is acceptable and unacceptable, and are testing the leader. Putting the leader into a typically authoritarian role can permit the individual, or group, to slide along relatively uninvolved. They will engage in obsessing (that is, repeating issues which could be important, but are not dealt with) in an attempt to force the leader to structure and impose strict procedures. They will complain, vacillate, boast, and refuse to take any responsibility to get the leader into a known role. It is of ultimate importance that the leader be aware of group and individual maneuvers and avoid these pitfalls.

Physical Activity as Tension Release

A high proportion of all communication between humans is nonverbal, and certainly we see the prevalence of such communication in adolescent groups. Boys and girls indicate their feelings and attitudes very readily by their posture and muscle tone, by their clothes, their make-up, their hair, their facial expressions, their gestures. In the group, they easily become restless. They are often like a flock of snow geese, rising, walking around, sitting down again. They will feign sleep or even sometimes actually fall asleep. They touch each other, wrestle, giggle, grimace. They may push their chairs back from the group, try to walk out of the room, lean out of the window.

Significance of Silence

Silence is one of the most potent means by which groups and individuals in the group can express themselves. It is also sometimes the hardest for adolescents themselves to tolerate because of their general difficulty in handling anxiety.

Two dimensions of silence concern the group leader. First, the group silence, and second, the silence of the individual member. Group silences can mean many things. They can be reflective, as the members mull over some experience or idea which has just been presented in the group. They can be anxiety-laden, as when everyone is embarrassed and resisting starting the group, or when the members reach a place where to go on would be upsetting. Silences sometimes have a dynamic quality, as when members are apparently girding themselves to reveal some very significant material, a silence which it is imperative the leader understands and does not break. Sometimes, after some solid work has been accomplished, silences can be relaxed, satisfied, and intimate. Again, silences can be extraordinarily hostile or withholding. Sometimes members are determined not to work on their problems or are very angry with the leader. Sometimes they are full of depression and despair, lethargy, or boredom. These are truly resistive silences.

How does the leader understand these silences and consequently know how to deal with them? He consciously or unconsciously observes all the nonverbal cues and is aware of both the context of previous discussion and the voice tones. There is also something else which is presumably an intangible composite of all these things, the quality of tension in the room, the group climate. No one really understands what is specific to this atmosphere. It may be that individual reactions of members create pressure, humidity, and electric discharge which have a part to play in this, and to which individuals are unconsciously sensitive. Silence for the individual group member can have many uses. An individual may be silent yet very actively participating. A member may be playing out a very typical role, or he may have essentially withdrawn from the group. Some people handle their anxiety by "going blank." They blot out and cease to become conscious of what is going on. Others become very sleepy. Still others daydream. These people are essentially not participating in the group, although they are present in the room. Their presence, however, may disturb and annoy the others because they do not reveal their thoughts and feelings.

Others listen. Sometimes they go through agonies wishing to say something, but fearing attack, derision, or exposure. Sometimes they are too slow in reacting. Others are eager to take part, but they become too emotional and do not dare express themselves. Some members are content to allow others to express their feelings for them. They ride along learning, but do not themselves contribute.

Two very interesting roles can be played by silent members. In one, the individual fantasies that by remaining silent he has more power than the others, for he knows much about them while they know nothing about him. Such an individual forgets the purpose of the group in developing a struggle for control between himself and others. A second interesting reaction is expressed by the individual who remains silent because he wants to be asked. He waits until the leader turns to him. Sometimes he fixes him with a demanding stare. He wishes to be treated as special and have the adult prove his interest. Of course, all these different reasons for silence carry role significance. The member who blots out the group or daydreams is expressing his difficulty in relating to others and becoming part of a group. He is essentially opting out and remaining an isolate. The member who silently demands to be asked expects to be treated as special and favored by others. Those who are afraid to speak expect to be made into victims, or are afraid of their own power to annihilate others.

Chattering and Horseplay

Chattering is very frequent in adolescent groups. The extent to which this is appropriately dealt with depends directly on the type of group. In groups which are largely experiential, the leader is most likely to wait his opportunity to open up more meaningful discussion. In groups which are task-related, it can be important for the leader to raise questions about the relevance of the discussion. Sometimes group members will try to shift the responsibility for making them talk about relevant material to the leader. The leader should not allow himself to be enticed into this power struggle for he can always be defeated. Teen-agers are particularly good at provoking adults into battles over control and responsibility.

Horseplay may serve a similar purpose. It can also be clearly a competitive and attention-getting device. In a group of 13 to 14 year-old boys, when one boy showed the leader a tape recorder he had brought, another boy immediately picked a fight with a third group member and drew the leader's attention away from the first boy.

Scapegoating

Scapegoating, one of the most conspicuous group mechanisms, is prevalent in all sizes and conditions of groups. It involves the displacement of anger and attack from its real object onto another. The most usual form of scapegoating is the transfer of anger from the leader to another group member.

The conditions for scapegoating always imply a difference between the scapegoat and the other members. In general there is a rule that the higher the degree of hostility and aggression in a group, the more likely is scapegoating to occur and the less tolerance there is of difference between members.

It is important to recognize that certain people are more likely to be scapegoated: first, anyone who emphasizes his own difference, whether it be his sickness, weakness, or superiority; second, people who themselves suffer from a high degree of hostility and anxiety and who thus stimulate anxiety and hostility in others, and particularly those who act in a provocative way as if asking others to attack or beat them; third, anyone who expresses openly impulses against which the group are trying hard to defend themselves.

While these members attract the displeasure of the group in their own right, in scapegoating they are only attacked because the members do not feel willing or safe in directing their anger where it really belongs. For example, a group therapist had to go to several conferences and left the group with his co-therapist. The members were very angry because they felt that he was putting other things before them and treating them as if they were of little concern to him. However, they were afraid that if they vented their anger on him he would abandon them completely, so, instead, they attacked the weakest member of the group and almost forced her to leave the group. Sometimes a leader recognizes the group's anger and unconsciously encourages them to express it elsewhere. In dealing with these situations, the leader should strive to understand his own feelings, help the group to express themselves realistically, and then work with both the scapegoat and the group to understand the interlocking relationship between attacker and attacked.

Differences Between Younger and Older Adolescents

There are a number of differences in working with groups of younger and older adolescents. Early adolescence is concerned primarily with the establishment of a sexual identity and with the beginning to come to terms with the need for an independent life. Late adolescence is concerned with the actual separation from the family and the making of mating and occupational choices.

In early adolescence, the individual often experiences a high level of anxiety and confusion, which is reduced as the personality is recognized. This results in the following differences between younger and older adolescents: younger adolescents are more unwilling to accept and recognize the existence of problems; younger adolescents usually suffer from greater tension and self-consciousness; there is a difference in tolerance of anxiety; there is a higher degree of motor expressiveness and need for physical discharge of tension in early adolescence; older adolescents show an increased ability to stay with anxiety-provoking subjects; younger adolescents are preoccupied with physical changes and comparing self with others of the same sex; older adolescents are more interested in the opposite sex; there is greater stability of relationships in late adolescence.

In view of adolescent resistance, it has often been thought more sensible to avoid direct confrontation with difficulties and to build counseling into other normal activities such as recreation, training, or even work. However, if groups are frankly set up for rehabilitative therapy, the following principles should be considered. Because of the unwillingness of younger teen-agers to admit that they have difficulties, it is not useful to press rehabilitation at the beginning of the group. At the same time, the purposes of the group should be clearly stated so that the leader does not play into and support the resistance of members. The leader might begin the group by the statement that the girls or boys are together to help each other with things that typically bother teen-agers and then suggest that the members might first like to get acquainted. Older adolescents, apart from offenders, are usually much more willing to recognize that they have problems on which they want to work, right from the start of the group. However, many adolescents, because of their mood swings, are worried about being crazy and have reservations about being identified as having special problems.

Younger adolescents, when they first come together in a group, are particularly self-conscious. Any new experience is an ordeal for them. It is often very hard for them to start. They squirm, giggle, and whisper to their neighbors. Silence is very difficult for them to tolerate, and anxiety tends to mount fast. If there is too much discomfort, the teen-agers will drop out of the group. Several approaches can be used to deal with this problem. First, the leader takes more responsibility to maintain the flow of the group and helps to relieve the tensions and to maintain anxiety at a bearable level. Second, the use of articles at the table, such as drawing materials, clay, models, or jewelry-making equipment, enables the boys and girls to withdraw into another activity in periods of embarrassment. As the group gains in confidence, the members can usually give up these props.

A more structured type of group has also been used effectively with younger adolescents and with adolescent delinquents. In these groups, the day-to-day adjustment tasks have been worked out for each group member, and then the groups discussed whether these tasks have been accomplished, and if not, why not. Materials such as stories about typical teen-age problems have also been used to stimulate discussion. These aids are not necessary in the later stages of any groups, and older adolescents can learn to work appropriately from the beginning.

In all adolescent groups, there is much difficulty in staying with discussions focused around the members' concerns, but the ability increases with maturity. In most groups composed of younger teen-agers, there is a great deal of chatter about mutual friends and day-to-day experiences which leads into short periods of very meaningful discussion. For example, a group spent some time exchanging names of boys; then one girl told how a boy whom she did not like kept on wanting to kiss her. How did one deal with this? The girls discussed tactics and then for a few moments talked about their feelings and anxieties, about being overcome; then the discussion was quickly changed. In a group of older girls, there is much more ability to discuss the problems of being accepted if one does not go along with the boys' demands and typical feelings about not being really loveable or desirable.

Sometimes a group resists attempts by an individual to deal with a subject which makes the rest too anxious, as, for example:

A: The only person I could usually count on is dead. I just want to be with that person. Last night was the first time my mother ever heard me say this.

B: I asked my mother if I could get my hair straightened and curled, and my mother said, "No." Some one was there, and I said, "See how your best friend will do you Miss . . ." and my mother says, "Oh, did you hear that?" My mother says that everybody corrects her.

A: Will you let me talk?

C: Whenever I want to get my hair done, my mother will fix it.

B: My mother can't fix no hair.

C: My mother fixes my hair every two weeks.

Here the members avoid the anxieties related to death and separations. Anxiety and self-consciousness are often coped with through motor discharge in the younger groups. Boys and girls will poke each other, put their arms around each other, throw things at each other, get into physical fights, leave the table to wrestle, run around or dance, rush out of the room when anxiety is high or if they become very upset. There is constant movement. The therapist has to decide what is to be permitted. Generally, it is not desirable to allow the teen-agers to leave the room because this can become a major resistance with the boys and girls running all over the building. The decision as to who sets the limits, the institution or the therapist, depends on the role which the therapist is taking in the group.

Such motor activity serves the purpose of relieving tension

and reducing anxiety. It is also a diversionary and attention-getting device. When one boy in a group started to describe how he had received three A's on his report card, two of the others who did not do so well started to throw pieces of paper at each other and succeeded in diverting the group's attention away from the first boy. The therapist then asked the group to look at what was going on and the different ways the boys competed for attention—by being good, pleasing, succeeding, by being disruptive during discussion. The boys who had created the disturbance were able to see that they were angry that the other boy was succeeding when they were not. The successful boys examined their feelings about having to produce in order to be liked.

In an institutional group of girls, one girl had betrayed the confidences of the group and the others attacked her. She rushed out of the room but was later able to return and face their anger. In a third group, the girls had spent ten minutes working on one girl's difficulty with her mother—who, the girl felt, disparaged her. There was a short pause; then one of the other girls jumped up and shouted "Who can do the twist?" The girls all followed and danced the twist to their own singing for three or four minutes and then came back to the table, and the discussion continued. Older adolescents will shout and thump the table, but are usually able to stay seated for the duration of the meeting.

Not only moods but also relationships to people are extremely volatile in early adolescence. At one moment a group member may be very friendly to the leader, at the next hating him and rejecting him completely. There is constant challenge and testing of the leader and a great need to have him be perfect. At this time of life, as parents know all too well, it is so easy to say the wrong thing or to phrase something in a way which infuriates the teen-ager, so that group operations are much less stable than in groups of older adolescents. Usually with the latter, once a positive relationship is established it remains a solid underlay to surface disagreements and negative feelings.

To complicate group relationships, early adolescence is the period of maximum interest in other members of the same sex. Girls and boys are interested in comparing themselves with each other, and intimacy and affection are often thought of as homosexual. In the American culture, this can occasion a good deal of anxiety. It also happens that, because of fluctuations between dependence and independence and the need for a model for identification, very strong attachments develop toward adults of the same sex. Both of these trends can be seen as homosexuality and defended against with intense anxiety. This can become a tremendous problem in groups of early adolescents and needs to be dealt with openly and reassuringly. Sometimes the group starts with talk of queers and much provocative and anxious giggling, which is a sure sign of sexuality. At this point, it is often desirable for the leader to comment that the members seem to be thinking a lot about homosexuality and that they might like to talk and understand more about it. If this is not dealt with, the anxiety turns into wild, uncontrollable acting-out in the group and can disrupt it. Adolescent groups become very angry and punishing if the leader does not understand what they are trying to talk about and if he evades the subject. The leader's own capacity to be easy with such subjects is, of course, crucial. The raw emotions expressed by adolescents often stimulate old unworked through conflicts in the therapist, and the intense and open anger or derision of resistive youth can be very hard to take.

Very intense negative reactions which can develop toward the leader as a defense against positive feelings are sometimes more difficult to handle. Often it is enough to interpret anxiety about closeness and to discuss the attachment as a desire to have an all-loving mother, a desire which no one can ever really fulfill. It may be that the conflict becomes so intense that a neutral outside therapist may have to deal with it.

Groups composed of older adolescents become increasingly more like adult groups. The leader still needs to be more active than in many adult groups in helping the adolescents deal with their anxiety, in presenting a model for identification, and in stating values clearly. However, older adolescents face their problems more freely and take more responsibility in setting their own limits. There is no need for crafts, and there is much less expression through physical movement.

While in older adolescence focus is on the individual's separation from his family, in early adolescence, particularly in middle-class families, the parents are usually deeply involved in the adolescents' difficulties. The problem is usually a family problem; the adolescent is made "it" and deeply resents it. Wherever possible, the family should be seen together in the beginning to place the problem firmly in the middle as a family problem with family responsibility. Parents should be involved in treatment and no promises made with regard to secrecy on the grounds that communication is usually a problem between parents and adolescents and that this is something which needs to be worked on. Experiments with groups composed of several adolescents and their parents show much promise in working out family difficulties. Essentially, the family system which pressures and conditions the behavior of individual members is, in this method, the target of change.

Termination

The termination of groups should be considered on two levels: first, the basic feelings and typical maneuvers involved in dissolving the groups; the second, how to manage termination for the individual and the group as a whole.

Whether a group has been meeting for only a short time or

whether it has been an intensive long-term treatment or social group, if there have been meaningful experiences there will be reactions to separation. Sometimes the group tries to ignore the fact that they are about to terminate. A second very typical maneuver is reliving the experiences which the members have gone through together. A third is when the group plans to meet again in what they hope will be like "old times." As the group nears its end, the members may frantically try to deal with all issues which concern them, withdraw interest, loosen ties, or express depression and anger.

While the group expresses these typical maneuvers, individuals may react differently. Some outwardly deny all feeling, others desire very abrupt termination, while others experience anxiety and temporary exasperation. Some members suddenly bring up an important problem which they have avoided throughout the group.

With short-term, time-limited groups, very few problems exist. The group has a set date for termination. It is quite possible for a member to have continuing needs, but these can be dealt with as a separate issue. Open-ended groups which members enter and leave at any time also present few problems. However, in groups where members start together and work intensively over a length of time, questions arise as to when people should terminate. Some members feel ready to leave but are reluctant to do so because of feelings they and the group have for each other. One way to deal with this problem is to set up a group for a specific length of time; then to review at that time those who wish to leave and those who wish to continue for another period. If a number of people leave, the continuing group is essentially a new group and new members can be easily introduced. The major problem to be considered is the difference in psychological sophistication between old and new members. Another way is to lose and add members as individuals are ready, facing problems of separation, reintegration, and trust each time. This can be useful for individuals who have problems in these areas.

If some members are going to terminate and others continue, there will be feelings stimulated on both sides. Members who are leaving may feel relieved, guilty, and anxious about their future, all at the same time. Those who are remaining may feel abandoned, angry that they have done less well. Intimate groups can be especially meaningful to those who have had difficulty in developing close relationships in their ordinary lives. For such group members, it may be important to develop ties outside the group to help them terminate more easily.

An important part of working with groups is deciding who should determine when a person is to leave? The leader can, and frequently does, make the ultimate decision; but, in general, the group should help members decide. Continuing discussion and questioning usually makes it clear whether people should leave or remain. Adolescents can be very perceptive in bringing this to the surface. It is particularly important that adolescents be encouraged to take responsibility both for themselves and for each other in coming to a decision.

For the individual, the dissolution of a treatment, learning, training, or special interest group means not only the ending of an experience, anxiety about separation, and loss of meaningful relationships; it is also a maturing process, a recognition that one has reached a new stage of development, learned new skills, that one can manage without the group, can do without its support, and has become more self-reliant and independent. Growing up, maturing, and becoming independent always involve a great deal of conflict and stress. This is why one frequently experiences a resurgence of dependency in the last stages of a group. During the process of termination, many important feelings are re-experienced.

It may also be difficult for the leader or therapist to give up a group or let a particular member go. In a situation where meaningful relationships have formed, he, also, must face and work out his feelings about separation. Being too emotionally involved with a member will make the termination process much more difficult than it normally would be. Leaders have to avoid creating the same sort of attachments some parents engender which cause panic when the child strives for independence outside the family structure.

It also becomes apparent during the termination stages of the group that there is a need for building in personal responsibility on the part of the adolescent. If he is permitted to remain strongly dependent on the leader, therapist, or group members, the fact of separation may cause too much anxiety for him to cope with. Should this occur, it will have all sorts of ramifications for the individual, the group, and the leader. The constructive effects of the group experience may be greatly impaired. Termination should be viewed as a time for advancement. The close and meaningful relationships of the adolescent's involvement in the group should not be destroyed; but aiding him in accepting the impending change in situations is crucial, as has been stated. The length of time and degree of his involvement will determine how difficult the separation will be. As noted earlier, it will be more laden with emotion in a tightly-knit, intensive treatment group than it would in a short-range class or counseling group.

The following illustrates a situation where one group member is not ready to terminate with the rest. The group was comprised of eleven boys in an intensive therapy program. It was institution-based. All of the participants were deemed ready for termination with the exception of one boy (Gordon). The decision to block his leaving created all sorts of difficulties for Gordon and his group during the two-week period termination was under discussion.

Maneuvers by Gordon took many different forms. One session he sat outside the circle and "sniped" at any participant in the discussion. The therapist, as is usually the case in such situations, received the brunt of his hostile attack. Another day he would be nonverbal, staring fixedly at the therapist and stronger members of the group. He would refuse to attend the group. On still another occasion, he physically threatened members and the therapist if he wasn't allowed to leave with the rest of the group members.

By the therapist binding his own tensions, and the group having concerned feelings for Gordon, this "acting out" behavior was important learning material for all. The group did not succumb to his pressure, and it helped reinforce the meaningful experiences. The group terminated on the assigned date, and Gordon became part of a new therapy group. His previous group had provided him with a forum for venting his fears and anger, but it is doubtful that he really wanted to terminate.

The therapist undergoes emotional stress as a group prepares to disband. Relationships have strong meaning for him, too. He must constantly guard against letting the gratification he received during the life of the group obscure his basic role. As for the group member, this is much more pronounced in an intensive therapy group than in a short-term counseling group; and it is hard for him too to give up a group which has lasted for one or two years and become part of the fabric of his life.

VI

Major Themes in Adolescent Groups

Identity development and confirmation is a vital part of adolescence. All adolescents are concerned with questions of who they are, what they can do, what they can become, how they compare with others of the same sex, how they can intrigue the opposite sex. They are likely to experiment in all areas of their life, in their talk, their dress, their interests, their goals; adopting new fads, making new relationships, learning new skills, seeking adventure, moving out from childish ways. Consequently, in any adolescent groups, certain themes recur over and over again. Teen-agers are concerned with career choice, dating, managing parents and other authorities, friendships, and feelings about themselves. They are often preoccupied with the meaning of life. They have desires to be both dependent and independent; they want to be responsible, yet free of responsibility. They long for a loyal and incorruptible world and for a cause beyond themselves.

Career Choice

The implications of any particular career choice are not usually clear to adolescents. They often have limited information on which to base their choice. When youth were asked by employment counselors to describe the life and work involved in careers with which they were familiar, poor youth particularly could only describe one or two.[1] Poor youth, minority groups, and boys and girls of all classes who are failing in school are

[1] Center for Youth and Community Studies, *Training for New Careers.*

caught in the dilemma of what they would like as against what is possible for them. For instance, a group of Negro girls, age 13 to 15 years were asked, "What do you want to be?" They replied, "Teacher, nurse, social worker, geologist." Later, they were discussing going to work and were asked, "What kind of job would you look for?" The response was "Cleaning or washing dishes, I suppose." The lack of expectation that their dreams can be realized is a great stumbling block for many youth and often results in their failing to try. Differential levels of education can also be a problem damaging to the self-esteem of the youth. A group of college freshmen who were having difficulty in passing their exams discussed how hard it had been for them to come to the university from high schools where they had been in the upper third of their class only to find themselves faced with failure.

A group of Negro youth who had tried to find permanent jobs with upward mobility were discussing the problems they had encountered in coping with the hard fact of discrimination. In learning how to become cooks, for example, they found that they were repeatedly passed over in favor of white boys who were brought in over their heads. They became very conscious that power and influence were vital factors in success.

Many youth who are in trouble have almost despaired of being able to develop a satisfactory life for themselves in any socially acceptable way. Their problems are reflections of this despair: giving up and ceasing to try; retreating into apathy and negativism, infantilism, or illness; hitting back at the adult world in angry defiance or delinquency; searching for excitement in dangerous activities; living in a grandiose or fantasy world; threatening to die.

Somehow the teen-ager has to be able to hope for a different kind of life and to feel that he can succeed. This must be related to reality, so that his own competences have to be adequately assessed and adequate planning built into the work with him. In the group, the adolescent can see how he frequently precipitates his own difficulties, can test out new ways of relating to others, and can plan new approaches to his life outside the group.

As we have pointed out already, Western culture leaves the adolescent in a very ambiguous position. Sometimes he is expected to shoulder adult responsibilities. Other times he is treated as a child. The teen-ager is very sensitive to this ambiguity and to his own as well as the adults' mixed attitudes. The following exchange illustrates this well:

Do they call you Mister at your job?

If they thought you were a child, they would call you Clarence.

I tell you like this, just because you are twenty-one, it really doesn't mean you are a man. You can be twenty-one and act the age of twelve.

That's right. Then there are some younger people who can act like they are older, like they are grown.

I think a man is a man if he accepts responsibility and obligation.

What makes a woman?

Same thing, a woman in age, but in mind maybe a different thing.

You think this group has been passing as adults?

No. Overage adolescents.

Relationship to Adults and Other Authorities

The adolescent will not be free to change his behavior unless his feelings about himself also change. The girl who is acting out the part of the delinquent because she feels that the family has cast her in this role can begin to act differently if she understands that she and her parents are each desperately longing for the other to prove that they are not a bad child or parent, but really care for each other. The interminable cycle of acting out can be broken from either side. In the following example, a group is examining how grown-ups and children nag and upset each other.

Sometimes you might bring up the argument and then find out that you are wrong and you don't want to admit it because you brought it up. You don't want to feel ashamed or embarrassed. Sometimes you don't want to admit that you are wrong.

I don't bring anything to my mother because she runs it in the ground.

Sometimes when I argue and I can't have my way, my mother will tell me I can't go somewhere and I follow her wherever she goes arguing with her, she will tell me to go on out and get out of her face.

THERAPIST: So, sometimes, you nag her just as she nags you.

In poor families, when parents are already harassed by making a living, tempers are often short and nagging explodes into physical fighting. Youngsters are upset and made tense by their parents' lack of control, yet find it hard not to reciprocate or to themselves explode in the street or the school.

Genuine respect and liking for adolescents are probably the most important ingredients in working with them. Lack of these feelings cannot be disguised; yet without such reinforcement from the adult world, it is hard for the teen-ager to like himself.

Youth are resentful of the fact that many adults treat them differently, as if they were children or not human. They feel very vulnerable because they are not accorded the status and protection received by adults. The following discussion expresses some of these feelings:

THERAPIST: What did you think the police would do with these men?

I thought he would take them to the precinct or something.

As soon as the teen-agers do something like this, they go out there so fast and track them down and do everything.

THERAPIST: You say they treat teen-agers differently.

They don't do nothing to those who are bothering them. Just say to stay in the house.

Like a teacher, if something happens and a lot of people get in trouble, it is all on you, so the principal is supposed to believe the teacher. Like I say, the teacher is higher so they take her say-so better than they would take yours, but I don't think that is right either.

Youth in poor parts of the city do not believe that the police are there to protect them. This is well expressed in the following exchange:

Does a policeman have the right to shoot a boy? It seems to me that a policeman is just like that. Can he do anything he wants to just because he is a policeman?

What do you think?

I don't think he has the right, but he does anyway.

Well, what do you think you can do about it?

Nothing, you can't do anything to a policeman except lay for him and get him before he gets you.

The adolescent feels acutely the suspicion and distrust which is prevalent in Western society toward the teen-ager. He is frequently in despair because the adult world has much difficulty in ceding him a meaningful role, permitting him rights as well as duties and really respecting him. In a program for the development of nonprofessional positions for socially disadvantaged youth, administrators repeatedly asked, "Can't you train older people for us?" Apparently they assumed that a man of 40 who had been out of work for years would be more responsible than a boy of 18 or 19 who had failed to finish school; a very disputable assumption. This in turn increases the adolescent's self-doubt and arouses his anxiety about his competence, his potency, and whether he can really be loved and accepted. Sometimes he gets into trouble because of this need to prove himself, to accept every test and dare.

These preoccupations are expressed over and over in the group. Teen-agers often start in groups to test the leader by exposing the worst in themselves. Implicitly they ask whether in spite of all these things, they can still be accepted.

In family groups, it is easy to see these mechanisms at work. Parents are afraid to allow their children to experiment. They cannot trust enough to allow the teen-ager to take risks and make mistakes. The teen-ager becomes angry and sometimes lives up to the bad image which his parents project onto him. In many delinquent families, the children blackmail their parents. They say—if you do not allow me to do what I want, then I will do something worse and really get into trouble. A sociopath cannot stand any threat to his omnipotence. When his power is questioned or his demands limited, his infantile rage knows no bounds; and in expressing it, the individual can push himself into disaster.

For many middle-class youngsters, the problem of separating and making new goals for themselves can be complicated if the parents push too hard for the same goals. In such a situation, the adolescent cannot feel free to go after what he and his parents both really want because he then feels that he loses his own identity and becomes his parents' tool.

These mixed feelings about authority make difficulties for parents and group leaders alike, for it seems necessary to be able to feel secure enough to set realistic limits for the young teen-ager at least, and at the same time have sufficient confidence and respect for the individual to allow him in the main to make his own decisions and to experience the reality of making mistakes. Essentially, limits should be explored so that their rationale is fully understood. Youngsters working as library aides wanted to act as receptionist at the information desk. The professional librarian did not feel that the youngsters had enough background to perform this job, which even beginning trained librarians were not allowed to undertake. The youngsters were angry and did not accept the decision. They met in a group with the receptionist and went over all the questions that had been asked her during the last week and discussed what it took to answer them adequately. They then decided that the professional's decision was correct. Teen-agers need to be shown, not told.

The conflicting feelings which the adolescent has about finding himself and about becoming an independent responsible adult, separating from his family, learning to live alone, and becoming free to determine his own way of life permeate all adolescent groups. From the start, the adolescent tries to push the leader into setting the goals and the way in which the group will work. If this occurs, his reaction then becomes, "You have made the decision. You make it work. I am free to resist." He both longs for responsibility and freedom and yet fears them. Limits are both security and hated bonds. It is important for the leader to be able to be undefensive, to be able to admit problems, to accept that he too can be wrong. The adolescent has mixed feelings about the leader's infallibility. He needs to feel that the leader is secure and strong, but it is comforting to know that he can make mistakes and survive. The adolescent needs to feel that the adult respects and trusts him enough to leave him free to experiment, and yet he too has doubts about himself.

Boy-Girl Relationships and Sex

The confirmation of the individual's sexual identity, the management of sexual impulses in terms of the culture within which one lives, the capacity to become intimate with members of the opposite sex, and the selection of a mate are major tasks and problems with which the adolescents have to deal. Consequently, all areas of the adolescent's life are colored and affected by sexual implications; and there is a need to talk about sex in adolescent groups. However, there is also a great deal of reticence about bringing sex into the open, for in Western society there have been traditional taboos on such talk. Thus, boys, girls, and leaders alike are often embarrassed and reluctant. It is most relieving for a group to be able to deal with sexual matters, for as an intimate subject it brings a feeling of intimacy and closeness to the group. To undertake this successfully, the leader must be able to feel free to allow the group to talk about sex. He must pick up indirect cues and indicate his willingness. If he ignores the cues, he conveys that it is not permitted to talk openly about sex, the anxiety is not dealt with, much anger and resentment are built up, and the group is likely to act out disruptively.

Often the first expression of concern is around homosexuality or masturbation. Teen-agers become aware of bodily sensations and are interested in comparing themselves with others of the same sex, yet are afraid of the implications of this intimacy. There are allusions to being queer. Giggling, teasing, and a high level of excitability are usually indications of a sexual undercurrent. Leaders should bring this out into the open, and such feelings should be discussed as part of normal development. There is both an affectionate, intimate aspect to these feelings and in early adolescence a comparative, competitive part. Boys getting together to masturbate are enjoying a new skill. Girls in becoming physically close are retaining their early dependency on mother and thinking about themselves as women in the future. If homosexual interests continue, the reasons for this fixation should be examined. Sometimes for girls it is an attempt to retain their mothers. Sometimes it is a fear of men; sometimes an identification with men or sometimes a need to be aggressively in control. Boys may have been very close to their fathers and obtained vast satisfaction from them. They may have felt it safest and most satisfying to be a woman or to be passive, or they may be afraid or rejecting of women.

Boys and girls in institutions often indulge in homosexuality or excessive masturbation because of the lack of other outlets for the expression of emotional tension in general and sexuality in particular. They may feel troubled and guilty about this. They may also, if their stay is lengthy, come to find sufficient satisfaction in these practices to be loath to make the change to heterosexuality.

Sex should be discussed as a natural drive and as part of human relations between boys and girls and men and women, recognizing that the other sex is human too, has fears, needs, weaknesses, and strengths. It should be emphasized that it is most important to know and care about each other, to respect each other, and to consider the other's interest as well as one's own.

Adolescents are very concerned about the management of sexual impulses, what kind of sexual activities they should engage in, and how they can protect themselves. Group members want to examine the nature of the relationships which develop between boys and girls, how sex is used by either partner, the consequences of sexual relations, psychologically and socially. Boys and girls must learn to think of each other as fellow human beings, each with unique needs and desires. They need to examine how they develop fully rounded relationships in which affection, mutual help and interdependence, intellectual stimulation, mutual interests, and sexual satisfaction are ultimately blended. They should explore the variety of relationships which can be sustained with different kinds of people.

By adolescence, boys and girls should be fully informed about "the facts of life." However, this is frequently not the case, not only because information is not well transmitted, but because when anxiety is aroused people do not always hear and understand well. Consequently, details of the physiological aspects of sex, the nature of sexual feelings and the sex act, and the details of conception and childbirth may need to be taught. Feelings about being a girl or boy, a man or woman, the implications of sex for the role one can play in life and how each individual can develop a satisfactory role for himself need to be considered.

Dating practices are of central interest to early adolescence. The following examples are typical of discussions in groups of young teen-age girls:

I don't want to talk about boys.

Sometimes, when I'm walking down the street some boy will come up and ask me my name and address, and I'll sometimes give my name and such and such an address that I don't even know where it's at.

One time I gave a boy a phony name, a phony address, and a phone number, and then one day I saw him across the street near where I live. I took off and ran because everybody around there knows where I live and my phone number.

In another group, the girls were discussing a first date:

Wilma, how old is he? 15?

No, he's just a year older than I am.

You're not supposed to go with anybody younger than you, are you?

Well, anyway, he came down here—he couldn't find nobody to go to the prom with him. And I said, "All these girls in the 9th grade, and you can't find nobody?" He said, "No, give me some suggestions." So, I told him the girl downstairs. He said he had asked her, and she already had somebody to go with . . . so he asked me, and I told him no.

You're a fool. Is he good looking?

Yeh, he's good looking.

I said no, then I said, "I'll think it over." Then I asked my mother, and she said yes, I could go. So I'm going.

Boys and girls in our society are frequently poorly prepared for the sexual stimulus of adolescence. They are given very confused guidelines by an adult world which refuses to face and work through the issues. Discussion has to be geared to the life experiences of the youth. While dating practices, containment of the situation, and delaying restraint may be the approach with girls and boys from protected environments, it is useless at the start to discuss them with teen-agers who have experienced sexual intercourse for several years. It is unrealistic to withhold information about birth control from such adolescent girls until they have had their second out-of-wedlock baby. However, it is important to help adolescents understand the implications of full sexual involvement, the energy absorbed in the culmination of intimate relationships which may be diverted from other essential adolescent tasks, and the consequences of the completion of the sexual act.

A girl of 14 who has sexual intercourse without taking any precautions is asking to have a baby. And to have a baby at 14 when you are not married and have no means of support is very self-destructive. These are the realities of the situation. So, why does such a girl need to have sexual intercourse? Why, if she simply has to, is she not able to find ways of taking precautions? Why can she not demand of the boy that he take precautions? Why is she not aware that being known as a girl who is easy to get does not enhance one's reputation? Is the sexual satisfaction so great, so necessary that she has to present herself as the kind of person that she herself thinks is cheap, that she herself would not respect? How is it that the boy is not more concerned for the girl and the consequences of procreation? How is it that neither can really believe that pregnancy will occur? There are many questions that one should raise. While not denying the urgency of upsurging sexual desire in adolescence, many boys and girls who indulge in indiscriminate sex do so either because they are angry and they turn their anger back against themselves, or because they feel lonely and unloved. They feel they are nothing and have nothing, and that the only way they can get anyone to care is by having sexual relationships. The girls are afraid that boys will have no interest in them whatsoever if they do not have sex, or else they long for physical closeness. The basis of all this is their own lack of self-esteem and loneliness. They feel of no significance and have no satisfactory relationships. They feel they have no talents, no charm, no attractiveness, nothing except their availability. Often sex is not even very enjoyable, but rather frightening and strained. And sometimes the girls say that the boys don't want anything else. (One of the advantages of a heterosexual group in adolescence is that one can have both points of view.) Often boys don't feel better for having had indiscriminate sex with girls. Why do they have to have it? Very frequently, because they too want to prove to themselves over and over again that they are men; they have constantly to convince themselves that they are competent and potent. If they do not feel competent in other ways, at least they can be strong, masculine, and adequate. If they can get a girl to have intercourse with them without protection, then she must really care for them. Yet, hasty, exploitative sex can never be fully satisfying.

In the slums, boys sometimes attack the girls for excitement or revenge. Such attacks are feared, although sometimes provoked by the girls:

> I was out one night about 10 o'clock. . . .
> Were you scared?
> No, I'm not scared.
> I know, but there's a lot of things that can happen.
> Like what?
> I don't like to say.
> You'll only go so far, huh?

For many, it is hard to control desire. Boys and girls are moved by the excitement of the present so that no thought for the future comes to mind. Yet, sex for the teen-ager can be a great strain. It can be draining, exhausting, and encompassing so that there is a reduction in functioning in other areas of life such as school. Sex can often be a barrier to more meaningful relationships. The pressures and intensity of sexual demand can prevent a boy and girl from slowly exploring and getting to know each other and from developing mutual respect and trust.

The role of sex in marriage, the establishment of a family, and procreation should be considered. Boys and girls are deeply interested in how to select a life partner, what marriage means, and how one can be a successful man or woman, husband or wife, father or mother. They ask, "What is marriage like?" "How do you choose a husband or a wife?" "How do you know when you are really in love?" Troubled relationships at home make consideration of these matters very difficult, as in the following example:

JEAN: My mother and father fight all the time. I don't think I want to get married.

MARY: My father left home, and now my mother has to support all of us children.

The management of roles in marriage bother the youngsters.

LEADER: Your feeling is that women should stay home with the children and men should go out and work?

I don't agree. I don't agree. Because if a man only works, he don't want to give you no money.

My uncle—I live with him and my aunt—he works in this laundry, and he works in a night club at night. He gives me money every time he gets paid—twice a week. When my aunt stopped working, he wouldn't give her no money. She had some kind of heart trouble or something. But anyway, after she stopped working, he stopped giving her money.

Nobody in my house works—nobody but me.

Don't your mother and father work?

My father is dead. My mother says she is sick and can't work.

My mother and my father are not together, and every Friday I go up after he gets off from work. He knows to expect me, and he can't turn me away because if he does, I call my mother's lawyer and tell him he wouldn't give me no money. Every week he's supposed to give us an allowance—me and my three sisters.

Teen-agers are often disillusioned by the difficulties which grown men and women have in getting along together. Adolescents, whether from poor or rich families, feel scornful and angry when parents preach faithfulness and self-control, yet act promiscuously themselves. The well-to-do youngster may have to contend with one parent and the problems of working out relationships with parents who are divorced and remarried. Poor youth cope with their mother's boy friends who leave or are thrust out when living gets rough. They ask desperately how they can meet and identify boys and girls who will make good mates and how to manage more successfully than their parents. Their ideals remain those stated by American society, but their expectations are that they will end up like their parents.

The Management of Feelings

In the groups, the youth struggle to learn how to deal more effectively with their emotions, to lay out the issues and cope realistically with their problems. The following illustrate one or two of these discussions. In the first, the group discusses how they deal with anger:

Sometimes when I get real mad, I get tired of doing the same thing over and over again. I try to change it, but I can't do anything about it.

THERAPIST: Do you cry?

Sometimes. Just feel bad about everything I am doing. I don't know, some things make me want to cry.

THERAPIST: When you fuss and then talk to yourself and cry, do you girls feel better afterwards?

I do; sometimes I do.

Well, if I get mad and I argue with my sister—she's older than me—just seems like she is always right.

My mother hollers at me—she made me mad, so then I told her I was going to leave home if she kept on hollering at me, but she knew I wasn't. So most of the time I just go somewhere and cool off.

THERAPIST: How do you cool off?

Go somewhere and sit, put on an ugly look; you think about it, but you don't say nothing.

In the second illustration, a girl describes the difference between feeling and acting her rage:

If you do something and something happens, you shouldn't put the blame on somebody else. Like I'm saying, if you want to go somewhere real bad and you can't; like she had to take care of her little sister, maybe she had the urge to put her in the closet.

THERAPIST: You are saying, as long as you take the responsibility. . . .

I don't think that is right for you to let your urge like locking somebody in the closet or pushing somebody over a bridge or something like that. Suppose somebody had the same urge to do you like that. You wouldn't want them to do you like that.

THERAPIST: So, it is natural to feel mad enough to kill somebody, but it not right to do it.

Not in a case like this—because I have a real bad nasty attitude, real bad temper, too. I wouldn't really do it, but I feel like it.

In this third example, the leader tries to help the group understand the way they deal with anxiety:

LEADER: I'm interested in what you said about you all making me mad by giggling. I think giggling can mean all sorts of things.

You mean you're not mad with us?

LEADER: I just wanted to say that I'm interested in why you giggle. I noticed that when you started to talk about death, you started to giggle, too. I think sometimes when people get anxious they giggle—it can mean all sorts of things.

Do you know why I giggled when we were talking about death?

LEADER: No.

To get it out of my head. I can't stand to hear about nobody dying.

Middle-class youth are presented mainly with the difficulties of competing with successful parents, with the meaninglessness of dedication to economic affluence, and the mixed feelings engendered by too tight control and possessiveness. On the street in slum areas, youth are faced with daily violence in sex and fighting. Fighting is used to settle disputes, obtain revenge, and as part of maturing behavior. Sometimes physical fighting replaces intellectual argument and depression as a means of overcoming boredom:

JEAN: We were on a picnic. Weren't nothing to do so I just ate up people's food. Messed up people's food.

M-1: Suppose a fight broke out, you would have liked that, though.

JEAN: You know my teacher said anytime there is a fight I am going to be there. I just like to watch fights, I try to push a fight if I can.

THERAPIST: Why do you think Jean likes to see if she can start something?

M-1: I guess she don't have nothing else to do. So she looks for some kind of excitement.

THERAPIST: So there is nothing you want to do, and you get bored and then make trouble?

M-1: Yeah, I get the same way.

THERAPIST: Doesn't this get you a reputation for trouble?

M-1: Uh huh—everybody fights. Everyone on the whole street—that's what everybody does.

While fighting is more frequent in the slums, thoughts of suicide are not uncommon among middle-class youth. The following is a discussion between some girls who had all experienced despair and had attempted to take their lives:

JOAN: My mother is never at home. She comes back from work, is mad because dinner's not on the table. Leaves me to baby sit the kids while off again she goes. I can't stand it. I don't want to live. Last week I took 50 aspirins, but they took me to the hospital and pumped out my stomach. I didn't want to come here. It's no use.

MARY: I've felt that way, too. Nothing I ever did was right. I was caught in a trap. There was no way out. Somehow now I feel better—I don't upset Mom so much, and she's nicer to me.

HELEN: In April when the lilacs bloom. That's a trouble month for me. Spring—everything should be so good, but there seems no hope.

The Peer Group and the Law

In both slums and suburbs, young men who do not feel adequate in other ways are fascinated by the excitement of stealing cars, for the car becomes a symbol of potency. Girls express their need for love, their daring, and their resentment in stealing from the store.

In this discussion, some girls give a few of their reasons for stealing:

Some people see something they want so bad and maybe they didn't have the money for it and they probably never have the money for it, so it gets on their mind and they take it.

Last year my girl friend and I, we used to hook school a lot and sometime we go to the grocery store and steal a whole lot of food, you know, we used to steal it and all like that.

When I steal, I don't feel guilty. I just feel nervous and scared after I do it.

LEADER: What do some of you others feel?

Sometimes I steal because I am mad, and I don't care if I do get caught.

I know I couldn't say nothing cause I used to steal, too. Go in the store and see something I want, I would go on and take it. I know what made me stop—I got caught.

Yes, it's wrong, but I guess they don't think about it anyway as long as it gives them a little bit of enjoyment.

Attitudes against squealing are very strong. The first of the following discussions deals with the retribution meted out to squealers; in the second, the group struggles with a problem around squealing:

Like if a boy gets hurt and he tells on that gang, then the gang is going to beat him again, like my brother—see, he was going with this girl, so she started going with this gang called the Pinder gang, so she told the boy something about my brother, so this whole bunch of boys jumped my brother and he got . . . he didn't tell the police what happened, his friend told the police so the boys were put away, and when they came back, they were going to beat the boys who told the police on them.

MR. JONES: What do you guys say? Each of you individually?

JIMMY: You mean if we were in his place?

HARRY: I don't know, that would be a hard decision. If you are going to bust down on your friends or not.

HENRY: I ain't going to point the finger at nobody.

MR. JONES: Do we have responsibility for something like this?

(Silence)

MR. JONES: Is there a right or wrong thing to do? In this case, is there? I just want your opinions.

JIMMY: Actually, the right thing is to bust down on them.

MARK: It would get out he's a "squealer." If you bust down, they don't want any part of you.

JIMMY: They might go out and rob a store or something. How would you feel if you knew these guys had guns looking for you?

MR. JONES: Scared and unsafe. But, whose responsibility is it? Just the Probation Officer's or everybody's?

JIMMY: Mr. Jones, I think it's everybody's responsibility.

HARRY: But Joe don't know what to do.

MARK: I don't know. I think I would keep my mouth shut. It's not my duty to turn them in.

HENRY: I would turn them in if they hurt my mother or something like that.

KEN: If Mr. Jones gets into it, they probably will.

JOE: I don't have to tell the police. I just make it clear that I don't want anybody's name discussed or mentioned.

Attitudes toward the law are generally pragmatic, as the following discussion illustrates:

S: You shouldn't break the law because you will be caught and punished.

C: What is "breaking the law?"

s: It means that you do something wrong, then you are caught and punished.

c: Are you breaking the law if you cross the street against the red light if nobody is in sight and you are all alone at 3 o'clock in the morning?

s: No! Only a fool would stand all alone waiting for the light to change. The lights were put there to stop if there are other people there, too.

c: Is that the way the law reads, or is that the way it makes more sense?

s: I don't know what the law reads, but it's stupid to stand there all alone waiting for the light to change. If you cross the street, you don't hurt anybody, and nobody knows about it, anyway.

c: Suppose a man steals from another, and nobody misses the stolen article and the police don't even know about it, would that be breaking the law?

s: No, if you don't get caught, that's not breaking the law.

Loyalty to friends and relatives is important, and the youth stick together and give each other mutual support.

Do you have a real good friend that you can count on for anything? Well, suppose somebody was going to jump on a good friend of yours who didn't know anything about fighting. I don't really like to fight myself; but when I have to, I do. Suppose somebody jumped your sister, girl, ten or eleven boys jumped your sister? (Yelling) What would you do?

Jump in, too.

That's right.

One time some boys jumped my sister, and I was scared of them at first; but when one slapped my sister, I beat this boy up. I said, "Don't you never put your hands on my sister again," and he never did, and that's been since last year.

Somehow the youth struggle to make a life which is meaningful and satisfying. Group discussions which are related to helping the youth cope more adequately and which are built into a variety of supportive sources can help in ventilating emotions and facing reality.

The use of groups in a number of different settings will be discussed in the next chapter.

VII

Groups in Different Settings

Groups whose main function is to increase individual capacity for socialization are usually voluntary. Groups which accent the rehabilitative or corrective aspect of social learning more often fall at the other end of the scale, under some degree of compulsion from an authority. The following listing of group affiliates illustrates such a continuum: (1) loosely organized recreation and playground groups; (2) school classroom discussion and counseling groups; (3) social group work agency clubs in settlement houses and "Y's"; (4) summer camps and residential schools; (5) aide or job training groups; (6) psychiatric, guidance, and casework agency groups; (7) groups organized by school authorities for rehabilitative purposes; (8) groups organized by juvenile courts for youth found involved in misdemeanors but able to remain in the community on probation; (9) detention home groups for youth beyond control; (10) groups organized in county and state facilities for the juvenile offender; (11) groups for adolescent psychiatric inpatients or for the mental retardate.

If an adolescent is able to maintain himself in (1), (2), and (3), he usually never sees (4), (5), and so on. If he "fails" at the first grouping, (4), (5), and (6), if available, can come to his aid. Should these steps fail, he moves down the scale to groups where attendance and participation will be deemed mandatory by authorities, (7), (8), and (9). And should there be total breakdown in his control system and the ability of the authorities to engage whatever strengths he possesses in a constructive way, (10) and (11) can house him outside the community.

A youth may come to a group because he must, because he wants to, or because he gains some satisfaction other than the stated purpose of the group; but the individual must perceive a need for change and begin to want something different before the group can be truly helpful to him. Thus, any captive group must become voluntary in spirit, a process brought about by a shift from diffuse self-defeating hostility and acting out to self-motivation for change, before any significant change in behavior can take place.

It is obvious that in the setting of the school, the recreation center, the clinic, the remedial school, or detention center a variety of groups can be conducted. As we have previously discussed, groups can be organized at different levels and for different purposes: information and orientation groups; groups which focus on specific issues and which clarify alternatives, feelings, and consequences of different courses of action; groups in which the major emphasis is on changing certain aspects of personality, such as the self-esteem, the ego-ideal of the individual, the general pattern of coping with anxiety-provoking situations; and groups built into other activities. Individuals may be reached in many different ways: through the peer group, through emphasis on the family, through emphasis on specific individual needs such as dependency and identification, and through focusing on how group members deal with a particular problem.

Recreation

Recreation outside the family and the school is certainly the most important institution in Western society for the personality development, socialization, and education of youth. Every play activity carries potential for improved self-esteem, the cultivation of sound interpersonal relationships, skill development, and for broadening general knowledge of the world.

The purpose of the recreational program may vary. Primary concern and emphasis may be placed on affecting the climate or values of the target community or group, on helping the individual develop himself and his relationships, or on carrying out the recreational program itself. Church and settlement house programs as opposed to scouting and special interest groups [1,2] have often attempted to influence the neighborhood as well as the individual by bringing a large proportion of the local youth into the program. Programs have also varied as to the degree to which the conduct of the group is structured and activities preplanned, as to whether the members participate in planning as well as carrying out of program, and the amount of conformity to the rules and standards of the group which is demanded of its members. Many poor youth and many delinquent, defiant, individualistic, or disturbed youth have found themselves excluded on this last point. For example, the scouting movement, which is highly structured and which emphasizes character development and performance, demands obedience to the rules, regular attendance, and has in the past insisted on parent participation. Some settlement houses and social group work programs which have been organized as clubs with formal dues, structured committees, set programs, and rigid behavioral and attendance requirements have foundered on the conflict between saving the "good guys" or the "bad."

In order to reach the "bad" youth excluded from socially conforming groups, detached workers and roving leaders [3] have moved out to the gang to offer them any kind of assistance or program which they will accept and to attempt to influence the

---

[1] Konopka, *Social Group Work: A Helping Process.*

[2] Boy Scouts of America, *Boy Scout Manual: A Handbook for Boy Scouts.*

[3] New York City Youth Board, *Reaching the Unreached.*

youth directly or to affect the youth through changing the anti-social nature of the group culture.

In the past, public recreation, particularly in low-income areas, has generally been an unexploited tool. It has performed either a passive custodial role providing space, equipment, and supervision, or stimulated "spectator" activities in which only a few could take part. However, there is a movement on foot today to form more intimate, smaller recreation groups in neighborhood centers, sometimes led by paid and trained neighborhood adults or youth leaders under professional supervision, and thus affect the neighborhood, work with the individual, and provide a variety of opportunities for the acquisition of new skills.[4]

In these groups, the members choose and plan their own activities with stimulation from the leader. They are expected to help each other and to work out any difficulties which arise among them. Although an active and varied program is desirable, activity also promotes interest in others and a habit of taking care of materials. Active games not only improve muscular coordination but necessitate the ability to cooperate and compete with others, to risk success or failure, to work out conflict within the confines of the game. Sedentary games, such as Monopoly or geographic card games, teach a segment of formal education as well as give practice in interpersonal relations. Trips enlarge the youths' view of the world, enable them perhaps to see how others live, to practice the skills of travel, to experience the joys of exploring and discovering the unknown. Many young people, particularly from poor or limited backgrounds, are very afraid to move physically or intellectually into unfamiliar territory.

Youth should learn to savor adventure; and ways should be

[4] Mitchell et al., "A Mobile Therapeutic Community for Adolescents," *CYCS*, 1965.

sought to utilize the weekends and summers imaginatively by stimulating groups of young people to enter new surroundings, go camping, or travel. Campfires are wonderful places around which to review values and life goals.

In any such program, all members take part; and the more competent are expected to help the rest along. Competence, self respect, mutual esteem, and individual and group responsibility, along with the need to have fun, are stressed; and while competence is anticipated in the long run, problems and errors are expected in the here-and-now. The rule is only that they should be recognized and tackled. It is even more important that activities are not imposed by adults or a few selected youth. It is preferable to allow a group to struggle with indecision for a week or two while they learn the art of solving problems and reaching group agreement, rather than imposing a program for which members take no responsibility.

The leader makes clear the outer boundaries of behavior which society or the host institution will tolerate, but leaves the members free to confront the realities and penalties of going beyond those boundaries. He himself maintains certain standards and values but does not impose them on the members. However, they are open to scrutiny, analysis, and evaluation.

When program plans are made, the leader assists the members to anticipate situations and to practice how to deal with them. If the group wishes to give a party, they are encouraged to think through who should be invited, what should be served, what kind of dancing or games will be arranged, and how to prevent gatecrashers or undesirable behavior. Such a party provides opportunities for members to test out boy-girl relationships in a protected social setting and stimulates discussion of appropriate heterosexual relationships. Dancing and games are also remedial exercises; while dancing the "alley-cat," a popular line dance of the moment, the youth improve their left-right body perception and, as the dance speeds up, their large motor coordination.

A variety of activities should be offered, for each has its special value. Art offers the opportunity for emotional expressiveness, the encouragement to view the world more intensely and perceive uniquely, to master a variety of skills and media, to widen the members' knowledge of the cultures of the world and the life styles and interests of different people.

When youth are trained to act as leaders in recreation programs, they must in the process not only learn a range of recreational skills but must also become aware of human needs and development, individual and group functioning, and their own personal conflicts in self management. In reviewing the issues which will confront the children or adolescents in their groups, they must themselves work out their standards and values. While there are a few programs which enlist such youth leaders throughout the year, the majority have been concentrated in the summertime in residential or day-camps, thus serving a dual purpose of furnishing activities which are enjoyable to both youth and children.

Group Counseling in the School

The functions of the school are to prepare young people for social and vocational roles in adult life. The school not only teaches basic educational skills, habits of thought and application, and a wide range of knowledge, but also assists in the transmission of the values of society and standards of socially acceptable behavior. It provides opportunity for the youth to learn how to relate to peers and to authority, to select a career, and to affirm their sexual identity. Thus, training in interpersonal relations should be a significant aspect of the school's responsibilities inside and outside the classroom.

While primary attention is given to counseling with adolescents in this book, training in sound interpersonal relations is already the business of the elementary school. The elementary school teacher plays a vital part in socializing children. In the classroom, the children are taught how to apply themselves to learning. They learn how to be responsive and to make friends and get along with other children. They must experience success and cope with frustration and failure. The teacher also teaches the children the basic standards of society in regard to comportment, cleanliness, manners, and the respective expected behavior of boys and girls. Much of this is taught as part of the daily life of the classroom, although special groups may be needed for children who are having difficulty.

The teacher also, through her curriculum, informs the children about society. They read about family life, how other people live, about their community and different work roles. On trips they get to know their environment and can study and talk with people in different careers. These experiences properly lead into the children's own concerns with regard to their present life and their future prospects.

Counseling in junior and senior high school should be related to the following needs: personal development, social and family life and sex education, educational planning and vocational counseling, counseling with teen-agers who are having difficulty in learning peer relations or dealing with authority.

Personal Development and Human Relations

Both the formal content of the school curriculum and the opportunities for interpersonal relationships within the school as a whole and the classroom in particular should be utilized as counseling material. The homeroom can be the center for discussions on personal development and social adjustment; how boys and girls get along together; how problems are solved; and what is appropriate behavior in dealing with authority. Classroom and school councils are excellent vehicles for enabling youth to take self-responsibility and to put the democratic process into practice. Boy-girl relations should stem most appropriately from daily living and from family life education, and the sexual aspects should be dealt with in the context of developing meaningful and tender relationships. Both boys and girls should not only study what goes into marriage and parenthood, but also learn the skills necessary for maintaining a home. Opportunities should be provided for observation and practice in child care, possibly in work-study programs.

Literature and movies can be used to supplement this teaching. Discussions of adult life and marital models can be developed from novels which portray life in various cultures and in different parts of society. Counseling groups, perhaps called personal development groups, can be very useful in helping young people learn how to cope with their feelings, work out their identity, and relate to others.

Sex education has become an important issue in the schools. Sex is only one part of developing intimate, mutually respectful, and responsible human relationships and should be dealt with as a normal aspect of such relationships. The problems which are created in the American culture because of the confused and ambiguous attitude toward sex have to be recognized and somehow worked out. To a great extent, however, the problems are created by adults; and the responsibility for working out the mixed messages should rest with them.

The group members should also discuss the special problems of class distinction, racial discrimination, problems and anxieties about rebuff. The school should provide hopeful, encouraging, and reinforcing experiences for those who have had difficulty.

Learning Problems

Basic remedial assistance must be furnished to all youth exhibiting learning difficulties. Learning problems can be related to a variety of physical defects, to continued conflict or stress, to cultural deprivation, or to plain poor training. Problems in learning to read and count may be related to lack of early physiological experiences which can be compensated for by exercises built into the daily school and recreational life of the children as fun and games. Latency children usually enjoy the order and challenge to drill. Balancing is intriguing. Craft activities in which creativity is encouraged and criticism geared to the abilities of the child can provide many opportunities for improving large and small muscle coordination and perceptual skills. Trips, films, and discussions can enlarge the child's world, increase his comprehension, and stimulate his interest; word games and counting games give learning in skill and speed of reaction. Careful grouping can avoid any sense of inferiority or failure and can stimulate by offering a challenge. Formal academic approaches can be reinforced not only by programmed learning but also by planned recreation and special activity groups within the school.

Emotional conflicts may have to be resolved before the youngster can commit himself to learn, and a child who has despaired of success must be given hope and experience of small success before he is willing to risk again the possibility of failure. Such children may need individual or group psychotherapy or equally may be able to respond to gratification, attention, and success in a recreational group.

At all ages, boys and girls can learn through teaching others. The status and prestige gained from taking this kind of responsibility reinforces the need for the mastery of subject matter which the teaching demands. Youth can meet together as a group to learn how to tutor. Such discussions should not only include the transmission of content but also the understanding of human behavior.

Learning problems may also be the result of rebellious or despairing attitudes to the family, lack of self confidence or a reluctance to grow up, inability to handle aggression or to compete. When conflict with the family is the basis of the problem, short-term counseling with the family in groups may be the remedy of choice. In a family group program worked out by Kimbro et al.,[5] the families were encouraged by the therapist to face and delineate their difficulties, explore how the members dealt with each other, learn to express their feelings, consider alternatives, and try out new ways of solving problems.

To a great extent, discerning teachers should be able to deal with many behavior and emotional problems in consultation, possibly with a mental health specialist. A quiet word in the corner of a playground or a classroom may be more useful than many visits to a clinic. Homeroom discussions geared to some of the difficulties the teen-agers have in their confusions about themselves and what they want may go a long way to settle many of the difficulties which otherwise can be blown up into vast and insoluble problems. Counselors should also be available for immediate on-the-spot management of crises, using the Life Space Interviewing techniques developed by Redl and his colleagues.[6]

When boys and girls are in difficulty, questions must be raised as to whether counseling or therapy should be engaged in within or outside school. Counseling within the school has the advantage that it is easy to coordinate the different kinds of help and planning which are being offered to the child. But if boys and girls are already opposed to school and are perhaps refusing to attend, they may find it easier to respond positively in a setting which is divorced from the center of the problem. There is also the important question of stigma. So far as possible, problems should be dealt with through normal means. Special

[5] Kimbro et al., "A Multiple Family Group Approach to Some Problems of Adolescence," *International Journal of Group Psychotherapy*, XVI, 1966.

[6] Newman et al., *The School-Centered Life Space Interview* (Six papers with introduction by Redl).

classes and special treatments single out the individual as different and may affect his self-esteem. They mark him as having problems so that others react differently to him. However, if a child's problem is retarding the group, or if at a particular moment in time a situation is more than a child can manage, it may be temporarily useful to create a special situation, whether within or outside the school. It is also necessary to consider what competence is available. For occasional and special problems, it may be more efficient to send a child elsewhere for treatment or to employ a specialist who can consult with several institutions rather than work with one alone. Staff too have their problems. In order to develop a school climate which promotes healthy development, all staff must be clear about their relationships to each other and to the children. Teacher, counselor, and administrative roles need careful coordination; and staff may require consultation in order to work out problems which they experience in relation to each other or to particular children.[7]

Vocational Education

The purposes of vocational counseling are: (a) to enable the pupils to be knowledgeable about career choices; what they involve; how choices are made; what qualifications are required; what opportunities are available; (b) to help students to know their own interests and aptitudes, to make their own decisions, and to develop realistic attitudes to work.

Vocational counseling should start in elementary school with a steady building up of knowledge of what different careers entail and how one chooses a career.

The following is a description of how a vocational guidance and counseling program might be organized within a junior or senior high school: large groups can be used for the orientation

[7] Nash et al., "A Collaborative School-Mental Health Program," Ortho. Conf., 1967.

of students to different jobs and careers through lectures from people in different fields and through films.

Small groups should be organized in which the students themselves explore their attitudes to work and their aptitudes; plan trips to increase their knowledge; hold discussions with community leaders and personal employers; learn to assess the potentials of jobs and the conditions of the labor market; plan how to obtain information; practice applying for jobs; and learn how to present themselves. Role playing can be useful here.

Many matters have to be taken into consideration when planning a career. Apart from the capacities of the teen-agers, their particular personalities and interests should be examined. How ambitious are they? How hard do they want to work? Do they like to work inside or outside, with things or people? How committed are they? How important is a successful career? Do they like responsibility, to be creative, to take leadership, or are they more comfortable following others? Are they willing to move around the country, work irregular hours, or do they prefer regular routines? What kind of pace do they follow? What are their expectations of themselves, their self concepts? How do they feel about immediate as against deferred gratification? How do they feel about making decisions which may affect their lives?

Vocational counseling with the average teen-ager implies clarification of desires, needs, and feelings, rather than basic changes in attitude. However, with boys and girls who have been unsuccessful, who have no hope for the future, who are delinquent, rebellious, and infantile, dependent or irresponsible, the group itself can become an important reinforcing tool in helping the adolescent manage himself more adequately. Vocational counseling groups should initially be unselected. Later, if the pupils become more knowledgeable about what they want, interest groupings might be developed. The emphasis of each program should be related to the particular school population and the opportunities offered by the community. Counseling meetings could last two class periods and be continuous during junior high school, enabling the students to become knowledgeable about a wide variety of careers and also about what is available in their community. The guidance counselors might lead the groups to act as teacher-trainers and resource persons to the teachers and their pupil groups.

Work experiences closely linked to education and training can also help students know more about what jobs entail, make more realistic choices, and develop good work habits.[8] Counseling and classroom groups should relate to these work experiences so that principles about working can be identified, problems arising out of the job ironed out, and the practice linked to theory which is taught in a more formal manner. In such groups, the leader is both counselor and teacher. He takes responsibility for keeping a connection with the work supervisors; brings up difficulties in the group; helps the members deal with issues; struggles to identify principles; and works out what is permissible and why. He sets standards and expectations and implicitly transmits a value system to the youth at the same time. He acts as a resource person to the group, shows them how to obtain background information, and how to discuss the theoretical principles which are related to their experience.

If the students plan to continue their education, they should be enabled to consider the opportunities which are open to them, what different colleges demand, and the chances for financial support.

Whatever the youth wishes to do, some individual counseling has to be offered to make specific plans for each student. Counselors not only work with the youth but also with groups of parents so that they too can be knowledgeable about the vocational choices available to their children. The counselor must also keep in touch with local employers and higher educational ad-

[8] Montgomery County (Md.) Board of Education, *Work Oriented Curriculum,* 1964.

ministrators and must keep up to date with the wider national economic scene.

Vocational and employment counseling must extend beyond the school into the entry job and continuing employment, if either the school or an outside agency such as the USES Youth Employment Center becomes the approved organization. Many youth flounder because they do not really understand how to manage a job or do not know where to obtain continuing education or advanced work when they are ready. Linkages between education and employment need to be clarified, gaps bridged, and the information about them readily obtained by youth. In fact, some educators and employers are experimenting with the idea of continued education and training as part of the working week and paid for as such, so that education, instead of being confined to a few short years, could continue throughout life.[9, 10]

Work-Training Programs and New Careers

As a part of the attempts to prevent and control juvenile delinquency and of the War on Poverty, a new kind of comprehensive programming has been developed which integrates education, remediation, skill training, paid supervised work experience, counseling, and often recreation and group living into a coordinated effort to prepare youth to lead a successful and independent adult life. While these programs have been directed toward the poverty-stricken, the delinquent, and the school dropout, their model integration of employment, education, and job and human relations training, in which all components are seen as part of the paid working day, may well become a way of life for many in the future. They solve many of the problems related to how to remain self-supporting while advancing in a career.

[9] MacLennan et al., "Training for New Careers," *Community Mental Health Journal,* II (1966), 135–41.
[10] Levin, *A Proposal for a Health Career's Institute.*

The lines of thought which led to this development include the therapeutic community programs developed by Maxwell Jones [11] in community psychiatry, and McCorkle [12] and Empey [13] in corrections; the work-study programs which started out as work preparation for less bright students; the prevocational training experiences and work training developed by Mobilization for Youth; the recognition that many people learn best when faced with concrete situations; the reduction in employment opportunities for unskilled workers, and the demand for technicians and professionals as the result of automation.

Three programs have been particularly important: the Neighborhood Youth Corps,[14] the New Careers training programs,[15,16] and the Job Corps.[17]

The Neighborhood Youth Corps started as a simple paid work experience program combined with counseling—a part-time and summer program for students, a full-time program for drop-outs. It has gradually included more services until it now qualifies as a fully comprehensive program. Counseling in the Neighborhood Youth Corps is conducted both individually and in groups. It is work focused so that all aspects of the youth's life are dealt with in terms of their relevance for his career. Counseling is concerned primarily with helping the youth examine his desires, his feelings and attitudes, his day-to-day problems, and his behavior in the counseling situation itself. The group is used as a reference group, and all are expected to help each other. Collaboration between the counselor and work-

[11] Jones, *The Therapeutic Community*.

[12] McCorkle, "Guided Group Interaction in a Correctional Setting," *International Journal of Group Psychotherapy*, IV (1954), 199–203.

[13] Empey, *The Provo Experiment*.

[14] MacLennan, *The Promise of the Neighborhood Youth Corps*.

[15] MacLennan, "The Human Service Aide," *Children*, XIII (1966), 190–94.

[16] Pearl and Riessman, *New Careers*.

[17] "The Job Corps: A Dialogue," *American Child*, XLVIII (1966), Whole Issue.

supervisor is emphasized, the latter seen as a key staff member in assisting the youth to develop adequate work habits and providing a career model for him.

The New Careers programs, initially developed at Howard University, concentrate on creating new technical-level jobs in Human Services. They provide counseling, education, skill training, and supervised on-the-job training and experience. Built-in provision for remediation, continuing education, and career positions provides advancement even up to professional levels over a number of years. The Core Group,[18] the central medium for counseling, is designed as a reference group to assist the aides to develop a common identity as human service technicians, to work out difficulties which they experience on the job through pressing the youth to examine these problems and their own behavior in the group, and to teach them a basic curriculum in human relations and community organization essential to their work. The program sets standards, has expectations, and makes demands on the youth, while providing opportunities to meet those demands. The group leader, often a technician himself, establishes the ground rules of the program, delimits the areas of decision-making which are permitted the members, and teaches the members how to take responsibility for themselves and assist each other.

The Job Corps was established as a residential work-training program with two male divisions and one female corps. One of the male corps has been a prevocational program for youth who were functioning at very low levels academically and who required intensive remediation. This program was established and run by the Department of the Interior and OEO and was situated in relatively small (50 to 200) conservation camps where the youth worked on the land. The second corps of Urban Centers, conducted in large former army camps, housed anywhere

[18] MacLennan and Klein, "Utilization of Groups in Job Training," *International Journal of Group Psychotherapy,* XV (1965), 424–33.

between 1,000 and 5,000 youth and provided a program of skill training, remedial education, and group-life counseling.

The group-life counseling was designed to help the youth work effectively in the program, to coordinate its different parts, and to examine any problems which were arising. These large camps, generally situated near medium-sized towns, have been plagued by two major problems at the centers and one difficulty afterwards: namely, problems of size, community imbalance, and difficult transition back to the community of origin. Size makes it very hard to individualize the youth and promotes a lack of communication between group-life counselors, teachers, and vocational trainers. Problems often go long undetected. Size has also created the temptation to run the camps in authoritarian fashion, which makes the development of increased self-responsibility difficult to achieve.

The influx into the neighboring towns of 1,000 to 5,000 young men from poverty backgrounds created an imbalance of young-old, men-women, poor-rich in the towns and a shortage of facilities of all kinds. Because of the demand for numbers, time was frequently not taken for negotiation between Job Corps officials and the townspeople to lay the base for satisfactory collaboration. Career planning and transition into the working world were handicapped by lack of early energetic job-placement programs, negotiation with unions, and other apprentice programs regarding the acceptability of the youth. It was insufficiently recognized in the early stages that to train without jobs is to play games with youth. Problems also arose when youth returned to unsatisfactory and anti-work environments without sufficient social support. There has been the need to establish strong local associations of ex-Job Corps youth who can band together and support each other in achieving a satisfying and successful life.

A vital handicap in all such programs is the demand by the politicians for the "instant program," which the professionals seem unable to resist. In all these programs teams of technicians and professionals have been found useful; and the major part of group and individual counseling has been undertaken by the former.

College and Precollege Counseling

The transition from school to college and the stress of the first years of separation from the family often reveal problems in the immature student, both in regard to social adjustment and in studying. Students have difficulty in making friends, dating, dealing with their roommates, organizing their time, and finding their way around the campus. They sometimes feel lost and lonely or encounter a conflict in standards and values. Group counseling [19] at several levels, from orientation to the college program, groups focused on socializing and studying problems, groups concerned with identity problems and difficulties in self-management, courses focused on the issues facing the young adult, family life education and family planning—all have been found useful, as well as therapy groups for those who seek help with more serious problems. The discrepancy between the standards of different high schools creates trouble for students entering college from inferior localities. It has created the demand for precollege remediation and counseling and for such programs as Upward Bound,[20] which provide comprehensive summer programs for high school students who have the ability but have been underachieving. The youth are offered a stimulating educational program, remediation, a variety of sports, crafts, and trips, counseling around life, study, college, and

[19] Belton et al., "Group Counseling for Freshmen by Graduate Students," CYCS, 1965.

[20] Berenson et al., "The Interpersonal Functioning and Training of College Students," *Journal of Counseling Psychology*, XIII (1966), 441–46.

work, and the opportunity to get to know college students who act as their counselors.

In all these programs, the creation of a positive group climate which promotes taking advantage of opportunity and insists on respect and concern for the individual is crucial for success. Additional elements of excitement, enjoyment of exploration, willingness to engage in conflict and problem resolution, to risk exposure, failure, and unsuccessful effort are also important.

Rehabilitation and Therapy

When problems are too severe for management within the normal settings, several choices are available: to continue to treat the problem within the school, work program or recreational setting in special groups which are problem-related; to refer to an outside clinic; to refer to a special school or hospital; or to bring in a law enforcement agency.

Psychotherapy is concerned with the achievement of changes in the individual's psychic structure and functioning so that he feels more satisfied with and in himself, effects more harmonious relationships with his environment, and mobilizes himself to best advantage. All such change is achieved by the individual's gaining a new perspective on himself and his world, through increased understanding about the self and the environment and through new experiences. Thus, guidance can be seen as primarily an intellectual intervention, psychoanalysis a combination of experience and understanding, positive reinforcement approaches, abreactive techniques, and activity group therapy, both emotional and experiential.[21] All permanent intrapsychic change is made in and by the individual and cannot be achieved against his will. No change will occur unless the forces within

21 MacLennan, "The Group as a Reinforcer of Reality," Ortho. Conf., 1966.

him are on balance in favor of making change. At some level, the patient must want to mobilize himself in a positive direction.

When an individual seeks or is sent for psychotherapy, he must recognize that there is something which is not satisfactory about himself and his functioning, that he is in some way deviant, and that he is not adequate to make the necessary changes on his own. He must seek help from an expert and place himself in a dependent position. At a minimal level, he must accept the authority of the therapist or the therapeutic agent. He must agree to expose himself and to surrender some control over himself.[22]

Because adolescence as a transitional period is one of maximum insecurity, this posture can be particularly hard for the teen-ager. The youth is changing physically and emotionally. He is struggling to obtain control over new drives within himself which sometimes threaten to overwhelm him and which make him anxious about his sanity. He is striving to define his changing position in the world, to review old controls and values, and to obtain status as an adult on an equal basis with other adults. The acceptance of the patient-position can be viewed as going against the life force of the adolescent and is often strongly resisted by him.

It has also become clear that often when an individual is given a particular reputation, stereotyped into a certain role and thus stigmatized by the community, both the organizational structures and the individual's own feelings about himself conspire to make him live out the role. For instance, when an individual is called mentally ill or delinquent, people start relating differently to him. They expect him to be queer, dangerous, or

[22] MacLennan, "Group Approaches to the Problems of Socially Deprived Youth: The Classical Psychotherapeutic Model," *International Journal of Group Psychotherapy,* XVIII (1968).

irresponsible; and he is set apart and barred from many opportunities. In his anger and despair he may well accept the role, cease to struggle against the pressures, and behave defiantly in the ways which are expected of him.

The reluctance which adolescents in particular experience in facing the fact that they are having difficulties and are in need of help has been tackled in a number of different ways. Authority has been used to force the adolescent to attend the group and expose himself to treatment. It is then the task of the therapist to help the individual recognize and accept the need to change and to turn the contact into a voluntary one. Some workers, such as Westman,[23] have felt that this initial opposition to treatment can be used as a cohesive force to draw the youth together in the group where the anti-authoritarianism can be dealt with directly rather than acted out elsewhere. Other authorities, such as Slavson and Epstein [24] and Shellow, et al.,[25] have preferred, even in institutional settings, to allow the youth to choose whether he will come or not.

Attempts have been made to reduce the opposition to attending by providing rewards and inducements. Westman, in organizing groups of delinquents in institutions, arranged that the youth could miss activities which they disliked and provided refreshments. Stranahan et al.,[26] working with "hard core" youth, held groups in convenient places and provided gratification in the form of food, play equipment, and trips. Schul-

[23] Westman, "Group Psychotherapy with Hospitalized Delinquent Adolescents," *International Journal of Group Psychotherapy*, IX (1959), 275–86.

[24] Epstein and Slavson, "Breakthrough in Group Treatment of Hardened Delinquent Adolescent Boys," *International Journal of Group Psychotherapy*, XII (1962), 199–210.

[25] Shellow et al., "Group Therapy and the Institutionalized Delinquent," *International Journal of Group Psychotherapy*, VIII (1958), 265–75.

[26] Stranahan et al., "Group Treatment for Emotionally Disturbed and Potentially Delinquent Boys and Girls," *American Journal of Orthopsychiatry*, XXVII (1957), 518–27.

man [27] describes giving candy and pencils, but in no routine fashion.

In some institutions, cooperation in the therapy group affects the conditions of life outside. The therapist may have the authority to recommend release from the institution or dismissal from probation, or the group treatment may be closely linked to performance in school or on a job.

Mental Health Clinics

Mental health clinics include child guidance and community psychiatric clinics, family and youth counseling agencies. Most of the youth come in semi-voluntary fashion. They are brought by their families or referred by recreational or school authorities. A few seek help by themselves, and some are ordered to attend by the court as a condition of their freedom.

Many workers have found that the normal clinic delays and the long evaluation of classical psychotherapy have proved too hard for the adolescent to tolerate. Instead, they have made an immediate contact at point of crisis, during which a relationship is established and some tentative hypotheses set up which are tested and refined as treatment proceeds.[28, 29] Where possible, the intake worker is also the group therapist, and no transfer is necessary.[30]

These clinics deal with youth in crisis: when expulsion from school is threatened, a girl is about to have a baby, or a youngster is so unhappy that he threatens suicide; and they also try to

[27] Schulman, "The Dynamics of Certain Reactions of Delinquents to Group Psychotherapy," *International Journal of Group Psychotherapy,* II (1952), 334–43.

[28] Peck and Bellsmith, *Treatment of the Delinquent Adolescent.*

[29] Stranahan et al., "Activity Group Therapy with Emotionally Disturbed Adolescents," *International Journal of Group Psychotherapy,* VII (1957), 425–36.

[30] MacLennan, *The Analysis of Group Techniques in the Treatment of Negro Adolescent Girls.*

help youth cope with long-standing chronic behavior problems, psychoneurotic conflicts, and symptoms, and individuals whose hold on reality is tenuous.

Treatment groups vary from short-term problem related counseling to long-term groups which aim at deep-seated character reconstruction. Most therapists focus on everyday realities and experiences within the group, although a few writers, such as Slavson and Epstein, report working at a psychoanalytic level.

Whenever groups are composed of adolescents who come under pressure, therapists have reported a rather consistent pattern: [25, 27, 31, 32] first, a resistance to treatment at all; second a banding of the group members against the therapist, coupled with extensive testing operations, such as griping, boasting, feeling out what the therapist will tolerate and where he will set his limits. There is ambivalence about the therapy and the therapist and a testing of each other; then gradual, tentative, and often circuitous moves at self revelation as members learn to trust each other and the therapist and to use the groups as support in an examination of the ways in which they themselves create difficulty.

Grouping is important in therapy groups. First, because of the intense preoccupation with the primary identification as a girl or a boy and the need for comparison with others of the same sex, these groups in early adolescence should be composed only of boys or of girls and are usually led by a member of same sex. Boys tend to be very rebellious, seductive, or self-conscious with a woman therapist; girls very provocative with a man. However, some therapists who are very secure and comfortable

[31] Gadpaille, "Group Psychotherapy with Hospitalized Delinquent Adolescents," *International Journal of Group Psychotherapy,* IX (1959), 275–86.

[32] Thorpe and Smith, "Operational Sequence in Group Therapy with Young Offenders," *International Journal of Group Psychotherapy,* II (1952), 24–33.

in themselves can work very effectively in a nonchallenging, nonprovocative way with the opposite sex, helping them understand how to develop sound relationships between men and women.

Second, the developmental stage is important in adolescence, and should be considered with chronological age in setting up groups.

Third, the balance of the group can be important in terms of the ease with which a group can be led. Autonomy is extremely important at this stage, and defiance and rebellion are easily touched off. There is constantly the need to test out the strength of the therapist; and a group with strong anti-authoritarian indigenous leadership with no one in the group to counterbalance this trend can rather easily become a rebellious, delinquent group, united against the therapist. It is not always possible to avoid this constellation in institutions; but in outpatient settings, it makes life much simpler and therapy generally more effective if attention is paid to this.

It is also usually undesirable to include in the group a member who is very different from the others and likely to arouse hostility or anxiety. This member is all too likely to become a target for scapegoating, particularly if, at any time, the therapist makes the group angry.

In any outpatient setting, clinic, private therapist, or court probation, a choice has to be made between grouping youth together who already know and live together or to establish an entirely new group. The former has the advantage that the youth can help and support each other outside the group, the disadvantage that they may lead each other into mischief.

In the clinic, groups of youth may deal with specific problems, cope with the realities and trials of everyday living, or explore and resolve conflicts which lie beneath the surface of the adolescent's mind but which affect his behavior nonetheless.

Parents

When adolescents are still living emotionally as part of their families, it is often not possible to achieve substantial and permanent change without family involvement. This can be clearly seen in situations where there is a schizophrenic symbiosis, where improvement in the adolescent may throw the mother into a psychosis; where parents are disguising the emptiness of their lives or the intensity of their mental conflict by concentrating on the problems of their teen-age son and daughter. If these problems disappear and the couple is brought face to face with their own trouble, the marriage may fly apart, there may be an intensification of parental acting out, or there may be withdrawal from treatment. When a mother, following a separation or loss of a husband, turns to the adolescent for her emotional satisfactions, trying to draw a son or daughter to her to make a more satisfying life for herself, the problems at home will only intensify.

A variety of approaches have been described. In family group therapies of all kinds, the problems are placed centrally within the family, and the individual's reactions to the rest of the family are studied in numerous ways: the total interactions of the system (Brodey);[33] in short-term intensive crisis management by a team of experts (MacGregor);[34] in circumscribed time-limited family groups (Ackerman);[35] in a concentration on the strengths and weaknesses within a family unit and a selecting out of the members with whom it appears most profitable to work (Bowen).[36]

Couples' groups have been established where concentration

[33] Brodey, "The Family as the Unit of Study and Treatment: III. Image, Object and Narcissistic Relationships, Workshop, 1959," *American Journal of Orthopsychiatry*, XXXI (1961), 69–73.

[34] MacGregor, *Multiple Impact Therapy with Families.*

[35] Ackerman, *The Psychodynamics of Family Life.*

[36] Bowen, "The Family as the Unit of Study and Treatment: I. Family Psychotherapy Workshop, 1959," *American Journal of Orthopsychiatry*, XXXI (1961), 40–60.

has been on the problems of the parents (Slavson) [37] or as individuals (Durkin),[38] or as a marital couple in difficulty (Flint-MacLennan).[39]

In almost all situations where a single parent is very close to an adolescent, it seems essential to help that parent make a new life for himself. Groups of such people are very helpful indeed when parents focus on the problems from the start.

Many lower-class families are not interested or are too burdened to be willing to discuss their emotional problems without any tangible gratifications. In these circumstances, groups and clubs are centered initially around activities—whether they be recreational, surplus foods, cooking, classes, or even coffee clubs—which have proven to be useful drawing cards. In one ongoing experiment, Gibbons [40] has been using involvement in a preschool program as a means of reaching parents.

PTA's offer opportunities for reaching parents with normal counseling and for setting up groups to deal with such troubled or special situations as bringing up the mentally retarded child.

In recent years there has been a movement to bring the clinic in closer contact with other institutions in the community. Clinic workers may now conduct groups in schools, recreation centers, and neighborhood developments. There is close collaboration and communication between teachers, therapists, and parents, and an attempt to create an overall therapeutic climate in which the youngster may live.

Juvenile Court and Probation

The function of the court in dealing with the adolescent delinquent requires consideration. The court is first of all a confron-

[37] Slavson, *A Textbook in Analytic Group Psychotherapy.*

[38] Durkin, "Analysis of Character Traits in Group Therapy," *International Journal of Group Psychotherapy,* I (1951), 133.

[39] Flint and MacLennan, "Some Dynamic Factors in Marital Group Psychotherapy," *International Journal of Group Psychotherapy,* XII (1962), 355–61.

[40] Gibbons, "Day Care: A Mental Health Intervention," *Child Welfare,* XLV (1966), 140–44.

tation. Appearance in court makes it necessary for the youth to recognize that he is in trouble and has been breaking the law. The court must first determine whether the youth has performed the acts of which he is accused and then must study how best to help him keep out of trouble in the future through understanding the nature of the problem and deciding upon appropriate treatment. There are three phases: determination of the commitment of the offense, study of the youth, and his problems and action concerned with rehabilitation. The first of these is a legal question; the others are psychosocial as well as judicial. It is still an open question whether all three functions should be performed by the court or whether it would be preferable to refer the youth immediately following arraignment to agencies that specialize in both voluntary and involuntary treatment, reinforced by the authority of the court. Much delinquency is caused by unfavorable social conditions and cannot be remedied without a comprehensive approach to both social and psychological problems. At each stage, groups can be used during social study for treatment in the community and as part of a residential program.[41,42]

The judge has a range of alternatives at his disposal. He can dismiss the case; warn the youth; insist he report regularly as a reminder of his precarious status; have his probation staff or an outside agency counsel the youth; or send him into residential treatment.

Groups in the social-study phase can be used to confront the youth with the immediacy of their problems, to explore why they got into difficulty, to recognize the need for change, and to examine the alternatives open to them. The youth help each other face reality.

Counseling groups have also been used to monitor the lives of youth on probation and to help them work out their problems in

[41] MacLennan, "The Use of Groups in Probation," CYCS, 1965.
[42] Fenton, *Group Counselling in Corrections.*

making a more socially acceptable adjustment and to keep out of trouble with the law. Examination of values, reconsideration of their views of themselves as delinquent and deviant, and thinking through alternate ways of dealing with authority, frustration, deprivation, and temptation are prominent activities in these groups.

As an alternative to sending the youth out of the community, considerable experimental work has recently been undertaken with the management of the open residence in the community which is organized as a therapeutic milieu and from which the youth go to school or to work each day. The youth work together as a group to decide on the daily management of their lives and to resolve the problems which they experience both in and outside the institution. The group becomes the central change agent through the pressure which is placed on group members to confront problems and to conform to new standards of behavior. The group leader does not make the rules or set standards, but he continually faces the youth with reality and refuses to allow them to slide away from problems. These programs are in contrast to the more traditional hospital or training school group which is run by a therapist who has no close connection with the program of the institution.[43,44]

Short-Term Detention

Short-term detention is used to hold youth who are perceived as being too dangerous to themselves or to the community to live at home pending appearance in court. Groups can be used for the management of the units, for the development of program, and to discuss how and why the youth have gotten themselves into trouble.

Even in such a short stay, the program can be organized to

[43] Empey, *Pinehills.*
[44] Pilnick et al., *Essexfields.*

have considerable impact on youth. All youth can learn how to plan together in the organization of their units. Older youth are employed and trained as counselors' aides to assist in supervising recreation and tutoring in the classroom or in orienting newcomers. The residents' council becomes an exercise in democracy.[45]

Residential Programs

Modern residential therapeutic communities and rehabilitative programs have much in common, just as old fashioned mental asylums and maximum-security training schools resemble each other. The latter emphasize control, security, an authoritarian system, establish a hierarchical system in which decision-making is made at the top, staff and inmates are held dependent. A series of noncommunicating levels are established which are secretly rebellious and conspiratorial.

The new residences tend to be small in size to emphasize the interrelatedness of all members of the institution, residents, or staff, and the importance and significance of each person's contribution to the total climate. In such settings, groups of various kinds are pre-eminent—work groups, recreational groups, living-unit management groups, school classes, therapy groups, and groups which include the families of the inmates, all woven into a consistent therapeutic pattern. Comprehensive programming and gradual transition back into the community with the increasing building of links, connections, and supports and the holding of the individual responsible for his actions are the keynotes of these programs.

Particularly in correctional programs, there has been a movement to train the youth themselves to work as group leaders and

[45] MacLennan and Davis, "Group Counselling at the Receiving Home for Delinquent Youth," IYS, 1966.

therapists' assistants. The California Youth Development programs have pioneered in this.[46]

Institutional Change

All these modern programs require not only a different method of working with the youth, but also a reorganization of the structure and a redefining of the purposes of institutions. They require also that administrators, supervisors, and workers manage themselves differently, accept new functions, reorganize their relationships to each other, and face their own problems in working under these new conditions.

[46] Grant et al., *The Offender as a Correctional Manpower Resource*.

VIII

The Group Leader and His Training

The first requirements of a group leader who wishes to work with adolescents are that he respect and enjoy working with youth. He must be observant and sensitive to their moods and the meaning of their behavior, and he must be willing to reveal himself as a real and honest person. Because adolescents are often confused, the leader should be clear about his own standards, while open-minded and willing to consider other views. He should be undefensive, be able to admit when he is wrong, and to accept a problem-solving attitude to life. To lead youth it is necessary to have competence, flair, or attraction for them—life must be interesting to the leader if he is going to interest and hold the youth.

Beyond these basic personal characteristics, the amount of education and training which the group leader must have will depend on the kind of group which is to be conducted and the nature of the responsibilities which the leader is required to carry in regard to the group and to the overall program. Today there is a movement to break down the work of the professional into constellations of tasks varying in difficulty and complexity and to train technicians for specific constellations, thus freeing the professional to concentrate on those tasks and responsibilities requiring a high level of specialized training, background knowledge, and capacity to exercise initiative. The essential difference between the technician and the professional is that the former, if he moves to a different kind of group, will require additional training, while the professional has a background of knowledge and training which can be adapted and which enables him to initiate and develop new kinds of programs. At the same time, efforts are being made to link technical experience and training to continuing education and to employment advancement so that the technician can develop into a professional.

As we have seen, a large variety of groups can be undertaken which require different levels of knowledge and skill. An individual who has been specially trained does not need to have years of education to conduct well-defined informational groups. Much of the direct contact with patients in therapeutic communities will be undertaken by staff who may have no more than a high school diploma; however, their daily responses will be crucial to the effectiveness of the program; and many of the opportunities for informal counseling, individual or group, will arise between the patients or inmates and these junior staff members. On the other hand, group psychotherapy which concentrates on enabling members to identify the ways in which they function dynamically, the planning of therapeutic milieu approaches, group consultation, and the training of therapists all require a high level of education and skill.

It is extremely important that all group leaders, technicians as well as professionals, should have a knowledge of individual personality development and functioning, the range of normal and abnormal adaptations, small group theory, and the structure and functioning of communities and institutions. They must also receive orientation in regard to the population with which they are working and the goals, policies, and practices of their program. All technicians as well as professionals require training in how to observe individuals and groups and an understanding of their own strengths and weaknesses. Such knowledge and training can, of course, be taught at very different levels of complexity. In the past, general formal education has been given primary importance, with specialized knowledge and training second. Experience and personality have been much less stressed, so that it has been possible for persons to have received Master's degrees and even Ph.D.'s and to be considered professionals although they have only a very limited and elementary capacity to develop relationships and to work with people. If the practice were to become general of linking work experience, formal education, specialized training, and personal development into a long-term employment package with education and training considered part of the job and consequently provided for as such, then the professional could begin to function with much greater competence and his training could be concentrated on advanced work. Now the professional as well as the technician has to be taught the basic concepts and tools required for working with groups.

At the present time, most training of technicians is undertaken on the job, although there are a few attempts being made to design Associate of Arts and Bachelor's programs which include counseling with individuals or groups. Professional training in group counseling and group psychotherapy may be included as part of the general professional training, may be obtained at a few specialized centers, or may be provided on the job.

Most such training assumes that the individual has received a background education in human biology; sociology; psychology including social, developmental, clinical, dynamic, and abnormal; social anthropology; and elementary methods of research and evaluation. Specialized training is expected to include knowledge of group theory and management which may be taught didactically or experientially, group observation, supervised experience with groups, and some kind of group experience which focuses on dynamic operations in groups and the individual's own self-management. Work with younger adolescents and children also requires training in the use of play and craft materials. Whenever the professional moves to work with a new population, he must become knowledgeable about the specific characteristics of that group whether they differ in age, socio-economic situation, ethnic background, or in specific problems.

Group Theory and Management

As good quality texts become available, more and more teaching is undertaken in discussion which frequently includes an element of self and group study. The important questions of how to train people to apply what they have learnt, how to make abstract concepts meaningful, how to relate theory to practice, and how to teach people to perceive and understand phenomena and to react appropriately with correct timing have not been definitively answered. The material which has been outlined in this book is taught in group discussion in seminar fashion. The group members use their own group experiences and their own reaction to getting acquainted and to working together as a part of their understanding of how people behave and feel. For example, the first session of the course can include an examination of the mechanism of getting acquainted; how the trainer starts the group; what the members' feelings are about giving their name and something about their background; how they feel about being in a new group with strangers; what their expectations are of the group. In these activities, it is possible to begin to teach group concepts:

1. Members coming to new groups expect the leader to show how the group should operate and to define the goals. If this is not done, members feel deprived, frustrated, and angry. The less the group is structured, the more anxiety members will feel.

2. The more initiative the leader takes in setting up the group, defining the limits, and the more he takes responsibility for the good functioning of the group, the more dependency he fosters in the members.

3. If one goes around the room asking members to identify themselves, one can demonstrate that this makes them anxious and self-conscious. It is possible in this way to initiate a discussion of feelings about giving names.

4. Even though group goals may have been stated quite explicitly beforehand, most members come into groups with hidden agendas; and the early phases of groups are often taken up with an implicit struggle about what the group will really adopt as its major concern.

5. In this first meeting, it can also be shown how members handle their anxiety in different ways, just as adolescents do when they are introduced to a group. Some members take the initiative for they find it hard to tolerate silence. Others withdraw into nonparticipation.

6. The character of participation can be examined. In the beginning of groups, interaction is frequently concentrated between the leader and the members. In a successful discussion group, after a time participation increasingly becomes horizontal between different members of the group. Dimensions of participation are degree, spread, and quality. Even in a first meeting, the general feeling tone of the group can be noticed and the concept of group climate made real.

As the seminar progresses, many other phenomena can be demonstrated which are similar to those experienced in the treatment groups. Trainees are reluctant to expose their uncertainties, inadequacies, and foolishness. They have trouble accepting and facing differences of opinion. It is hard for them to trust each other and to develop the intimate, supportive, accepting, and explorative climate so necessary for full and meaningful learning to take place. They too exhibit problems of dependency and independence, competition with the leader and sibling rivalry, just as the groups of adolescents do. They too at times test the leader. They are reluctant to accept concepts, rebel against ideas, feel despairing, and are bored that nothing is being achieved.

Members play different roles in the seminar group, just as the adolescents do in the treatment groups. Some trainees work hard, try to learn; others try and take over the role of teacher; others remain silent and nonparticipant; still others expose themselves as the foolish members of the group. Although it is not always very useful or even tolerated by the trainees to go too deeply into their roles and defenses, it is possible to begin to help them be aware of their own propensity to take on certain of these roles. In the discussion, too, as case material is analyzed, many of the different attitudes that the trainees profess become apparent to them and to the group. In the seminar the values and standards of the trainees should become clarified, for it is important for a group leader, particularly with adolescents, to understand his own attitudes to the everyday behaviors and crucial issues which the adolescent has to face.

Such personal interactions in a training program draw the group members together and induce an intimacy which makes it possible to observe more clearly all these group phenomena. Because of this intimacy, by the end of the seminar it becomes possible to observe typical feelings which members experience around the breakup of groups and the separation from each other, the process of termination. It is important to emphasize whether or not one plans to help members of a group become conscious of what is going on dynamically between members, that dynamic interaction is always present in groups and should be understood by the leader.

While an understanding of group dynamics is obtained in this kind of seminar as well as in group supervision and group observation, it is useful for group leaders to take part in short-term sensitization groups which focus on experiencing and understanding the dynamics of group formation and dissolution.

Group Supervision

Just as there has been a move toward treating adolescents in groups rather than individually, there has also been a tendency to group the leaders together for supervision. While both these movements have occurred to some extent because of the need to save time, both have also been found to have very specific advantages.

When we supervise group leaders together, we enable them to share vicariously in each other's experiences; we widen rather quickly their knowledge of different groups, and we expose them to a group experience in the supervisory session itself.

In the supervisory group, too, we find developing many of the same phenomena which are observable in adolescent groups. The counselors or therapists in the beginning also have difficulty in revealing themselves when they discuss their groups. They too exhibit similar problems of dependence and independence, competition with the leader, and sibling rivalry, just as we see them in adolescent groups. It is consequently necessary to develop an intimate, supportive, accepting, and explorative climate so that full and meaningful discussion can take place. While manifest countertransferences and resistances are examined in terms of the adolescent and supervisory groups, they are not worked through at a familial or genetic level. Where leaders have persistent difficulty with any type of problem or adolescent, they are advised to seek psychotherapeutic help outside the supervisory group situation.

One very interesting type of experience to be noticed in supervisory groups is the re-creation of the climate or problem which is being described in relation to a counseling or therapy group. In this situation, the leader appears to play the part of the adolescent or group of adolescents in such a way that he stimulates reactions similar to his own with his group in the supervisory group. A therapist was describing how a group seemed to tantalize and to hold him off with isolationist obsessional mechanisms. They would complain and then deny their reactions. As the supervisory group tried to help him explore this problem, it became apparent that he was holding them off and refusing to reveal for them his real feelings in the same way that his adolescent group had dealt with him. The members of the supervisory group found themselves reacting as the leader had done by feeling tantalized, helpless, and angry with this shadowboxing. When this interaction had been examined, the therapist was much better able to deal with himself and his adolescents in the therapy group.

In general, such supervisory groups should be kept small. When they are too large it is hard to develop sufficient trust and intimacy, and one does not have enough time to examine in detail what goes on in the groups. For groups which are held once a week, a supervisory group of four leaders and a supervisor who meet for two hours each week seems sufficient. Each leader has a group which is reviewed and analyzed twice a month for an hour at a time. So that everyone can keep track of the groups, brief summaries on each adolescent are provided and the leaders write processed reports of the meetings on which they will report and summaries of the others, all of which are distributed and read before the supervisory sessions.

It is possible to set these groups up in different ways. They can be composed of:

1. Leaders who are all learning to work with the same type of group, such as analytically oriented group psychotherapy with neurotic adolescents or recreational groups led by junior counselors.
2. Leaders who are working with different kinds of groups which are interconnected, such as parent and child groups led by junior counselors.

3. Leaders who are using the same method with different populations.
4. Leaders who are working with groups where different methods are being used experimentally with similar populations, such as counseling and psychoanalytic groups with adolescents.

Each of these arrangements has some special advantages from the point of view of a training experience.

In method number 1. the leaders are enabled to gain quickly a wide experience with a particular technique, problem, or type of adolescent. Four leaders were supervised together who were all leading groups of unmarried mothers living in a shelter prior to giving birth to their babies. In comparing the four groups, the leaders were struck by the similarity of the content and sequence and additionally gained a very wide and intensive knowledge of the problems and decisions which the unmarried mother has to face. Several employment counselors working together soon learn the typical problems and attitudes of their adolescent clients.

Similarly, when four therapists were working with psychoanalytically oriented groups of neurotic couples working on their marital difficulties, they were impressed by the amount of pressure which each marital partner put on the group and on the therapist to try and get them on their side against the other. They were able to share with each other the ways in which they dealt with this problem.

This method makes it easy to see how leaders can react differently to the same problem and is helpful in overcoming resistance to looking at one's own difficulties. In one recreation group, the girls expressed their defiance by not coming to the table for refreshments. The leader, understanding their need to express their independence, remained relaxed and unconcerned; and very soon the children gave this up. In another group, however, the same problem arose; but this time it happened that the leader had had suppressed desires to act in this way as a child when angry but had not dared. She was threatened by the angry feelings which she transferred to the children, who sensed that they had been able to get under her skin, so continued to defy her. The leader was able, with the assistance of her supervisory group members, to recognize her irrationally transferred feelings. This reduced her anxiety so that she was no longer upset by the children, and the game of defying her in this way lost its interest.

Interconnected groups are particularly useful in work with families, where they enable leaders to gain an excellent picture of the ways in which different members of a family function and to build up a realistic view of how parent-child problems mesh.

When leaders can examine the use of the same method with different kinds of adolescents or problems, they are able to gain an excellent idea of the flexibility and limitations of the method. They can learn what is basic to the method and what can be adapted.

Finally, group leaders who are working with similar populations but using different methods, such as guidance and therapeutic groups of parents, can be grouped together. This enables the leaders to understand something of the range of the different methods. They can compare the leadership activities which teach a group how to function at a particular level, and they can learn how to select more easily for different kinds of group therapy.

A final advantage of group supervision is the ease with which the supervisor is enabled to move from specific to theoretical discussion. When a number of groups can be compared, generalizations are more easily made. Not only group but also individual and family dynamics are more easily and potently taught by this method.

While a certain amount of individual supervision is included in the training of beginning group leaders, it is increasingly becoming our practice to work exclusively in small group sessions.

Group Observation

The demonstration group which is observed by a group of trainees and a supervisor and then discussed with group leader and supervisor is an invaluable training device. It is possible to identify personal distortions and counter-transferences in action, observe individual and group phenomena and leadership techniques, and to discuss alternative courses of action. In such a group, it is also possible to examine and discuss the group dynamics which are operative in this as in all other groups.

Self-Knowledge and Self-Management

There has been considerable controversy as to whether group counselors and psychotherapists should also have taken part as members in a counseling or therapy group. In our view it is important for group leaders to feel the force of the group, to accept that they too have problems, and to understand their own strengths and weaknesses. It is important also that they are able to be undefensive, to be able to expose themselves in tackling problems which occur in their work, and to have empathy for the difficulties which their clients or patients experience in revealing themselves. Therefore, we believe that group leaders should be required to participate in either self-development or treatment groups for at least a year.

Audio-Visual Aids

Taped recordings of sessions have been used quite frequently both for self-study by the leader and for supervisory purposes on a selective basis. A limited number of films have been made and are found useful in teaching, such as Slavson's Activity Group Therapy and the groups at Highfields.

There is now considerable interest in the use of video tape as feedback both to group members and to the leader. Experimentation with this medium has been held back primarily by the cost of equipment.

Evaluation

Just as no program of intervention should be established without a system of quality control, no training should be developed without evaluation. We must know whether the training is proceeding according to plan, whether the trainees are learning what is offered to them, whether they are able to apply it, and whether the result is effective. This implies that all training programs must be well conceptualized and described, that at least spot checking of the training operations should be undertaken, and that the trainees should be followed up after they leave the program, as well as tested at its end.

Major problems in evaluating training as in evaluating programs have been related to uncertainty about goals. While trainers have usually been clear about the knowledge they felt group leaders should have, they have been much less certain about what kind of person makes a good leader or an effective therapist. Because of this uncertainty, trainers have been reluctant to exclude potential leaders on the grounds of personality except when there are clear indications of irresponsibility, malperception, or poor functioning.

Summary

At this time it can be said that the areas of manpower and training are in a period of change and experimentation. There are movements to differentiate less from more highly skilled tasks, to use new sources of manpower, and to move from didactic to more experiential training. Above all, there is an increasing recognition that the personality of the leader is a vitally important component in his effectiveness and that the setting in which he works will play an important part in limiting or realizing his potential.

EPILOGUE
The Youth Revolution—1970

Earlier in this book, we identified some of the needs of teenagers to feel secure and successful and to explore their value systems, their personal goals, and their self-concept. We have emphasized their tendency to reject old authorities and old values in the service of becoming independent and a whole person. We have stressed too youths' need to adopt a significant role in society, to belong to a group or a cause which seems worthwhile, to be and to feel respected.

We have also discussed throughout this book ways in which society and its institutions can become more responsive to the needs of youth. An authoritarian society simply will not meet the demands of today. Youth today are demanding a say in their own destiny. They are insisting on a share in deciding what kind of world they will live in, what they will learn, and what values are given priority. They want to be informed and to be free to experiment and to learn from their experiences. They are impatient of delays. Communication, respect, dialogue, participation and sharing of control, responsiveness are key words in the engagement of youth with adults.

We have identified too the problems and dangers which are created by rigid institutions. Many communities have neglected their youth, refusing to provide resources for work roles, recreation, representation on local decision-making, mental health services, and have put too little money into education. Many schools and colleges have been managed for the ease and satisfaction of administration and faculty rather than for the students.

Many mandatory courses have been dull and irrelevant. Teachers often have not taken the trouble to understand the problems of the students or felt any responsibility for helping them when they were in difficulty. Stereotyped expectations of students have had a deadening and disillusioning effect on many students. Technical questions related to the management of large numbers of students have enhanced the difficulties of building curriculum which really meets the needs of students. The tendency for faculty and administration and for government to meet protests and expressions of dissatisfaction with repressiveness and exclusion has led to an increasing tendency to resort to violence. From our knowledge of group dynamics, we know that when people do not believe that those in authority are listening to them or are concerned about them and when they are sure that authority will be unresponsive, then they will start to scream, shout, kick, throw things, shoot, and kill. Unfortunately, authority has generally been unwilling to recognize this dynamic law, to listen to youth, and to share control. There has been a tendency to stall, to play games, to pretend to make changes without any real intention of changing which inevitably leads to a disillusionment with negotiation and an increased lack of trust.

There are many ways in which the dissatisfactions with existing conditions are expressed. Many youth, challenging the economic materialism of Western Society, are struggling to achieve more satisfying relationships and a heightened quality of experience in their personal lives. Some have emphasized free sexual expression. Improved contraception has decreased the demand for continence. Many young people have insisted on the opportunity to develop full and complete relationships through coeducational dorms in college or through setting up separate establishments. A great many young teen-agers, impatient with the constraints of home, have run away to the large cities.

Drugs, too, have been used as a means for exploring enhanced personal experiences in the moment. Drugs can create exhilarating moods, intensify sensory perceptions, and cause the individual to regard life from a new perspective.

Drugs and sex are also used, of course, as means to reduce tension and anxiety and to withdraw from living. Immersion in these momentary satisfactions can create a cycle of exhilaration and depression which is hard to break out of and which stymies youth in the making of a more truly satisfying life. The demand for money to satisfy the urge has led many youth into delinquency and crime.

Some explorers, rejecting totally modern values, have moved out on to the land to establish modern rustic utopias which bring to mind the experiments of William Morris. Some have adopted new or old religions, astrology, or magic. Others have joined the encounter group and humanistic psychology movements which promote free expression, trust, and honesty through training groups, exercises, marathons. While these groups concern themselves with personal experimentation and change, others, more activist, turn to social issues and attempt to alter the priorities and institutions of society. Among these we find those who attack the role and functioning of the university, who support the rights of minority groups and the poor, or who battle for peace or a clean environment. There is much to be said for the position of youth in all these causes. If they are going to fight and die for a war, they should support its cause. They have a right to be indignant at the despoilment of the world in which they will still have to live tomorrow. Ideally, the university is a gathering of scholars and students, where the latter cull knowledge and prepare themselves for their future lives. If the students do not learn there what they need to know and if they are subjected to nonfunctional and unnecessary restrictions, inevitably they will be dissatisfied and frustrated. Societies vary in the degree to which goods and power are shared amongst their inhabitants. A society, however, like the United States which professes equal rights and opportunities for all faces a charge of hypocrisy if rights are freely neglected and overrun. Idealistic youth is easily disenchanted with a society which seems to put profit before people and which, calling itself a democracy, does not use the democratic means of representation, negotiation, the formation of pressure groups, and coalitions to solve its problems but rather resorts to force to maintain law and order.

The position of law enforcement agents is a particularly tricky one when different groups in society are in contention over basic values and the allocation of resources. Ideally, the police should be deployed to hold the reins and to ensure democratic procedures for solutions. In fact, the police and other law enforcement agencies are utilized in the service of those in power to maintain present values and resource distribution. Further, the law enforcement institutions are organized in an authoritarian rather than in a democratic model and attract personnel who tend to be conservative, authoritarian, and identified with authority. Consequently, we find, repeatedly, law enforcement agents resorting to violence and in many ways deeming themselves as exempt from the law, in their attempts to maintain order.

Another major trend amongst youth today is to organize to help themselves and each other. This is exemplified in the gang leaders in the big cities who have turned themselves into business corporations and employment agencies. Some youth have formed teen patrols to maintain order. Others have set up hot lines, teen exchanges, and information centers through which boys and girls who are in trouble can seek help first from youth of their own age. These organizations generally possess professional adults who act as resource consultants, trainers, and links with more traditional service agencies. Many youth who are suspicious and distrustful feel safer in approaching an organization run by other teen-agers than in making contact directly with the adult world.

Youth groups have also begun to establish homes and free

clinics where lost and runaway young people can recover and find ways to reconnect with society.

Youth together with less traditional teachers have established free schools and universities where they can control the faculty and ensure that the courses are relevant and in some instances teach the courses themselves.

All these positive moves are healthy, vital, and dynamic. The tendency of adults to fear youth, to keep them dependent, to repress and hold them down is as unhealthy as the tendency of some youth in their despair to become violent, to withdraw into drugs, or to commit suicide. A viable society must constantly struggle to engage all its people in making known and satisfying their needs to the greatest possible extent. No one will get everything he wants nor everything he wants as soon as he wants it. Everyone should feel considered.

The widespread understanding of individual, group, institutional, and community dynamics is vital to a well-functioning democratic society. Our institutions should model democracy, and our people should be taught how to make it work. It is not easy to achieve a satisfying life or a functioning democracy. Both are possible only if people are willing to engage with each other, to address themselves to solving problems, and to restrain their own impatience.

Bibliography

Ackerman, N. W. "An Experiment in the Treatment of Adolescent Boys and Girls," American Group Therapy Association, 4th Conference, 1947.

———— The Psychodynamics of Family Life. New York, Basic Books, 1958.

Ackley, Ethel G., and Beverly R. Fliegal. "A Social Work Approach to Street-Corner Girls," Social Work, V (1960), 27.

Aichhorn, A. Wayward Youth. New York, Viking, 1935.

Alissi, Peter. "Social Influences on Group Values," Social Work, X (1965).

Annesley, P. T. "Group Psychotherapy in an Adolescent Psychiatric Unit," International Journal of Social Psychiatry, IX (1964), 283.

Arnold, William R. "The Concept of Gang," Sociology Quarterly, VII (1966), 59–75.

Astrachan, N. "Group Psychotherapy with Mentally Retarded Female Adolescents and Adults," American Journal of Mental Deficiency, LX (1955), 152.

Axelrod, Pearl L., et al. "Experiment in Group Psychotherapy with Shy Adolescent Girls," American Journal of Orthopsychiatry, XIV (1944), 616.

Bales, R. F. Interaction Process Analysis. Cambridge, Addison-Wesley, 1953.

Becker, B., et al. "Adolescent Group Psychotherapy: A Community Health Program," International Journal of Group Psychotherapy, VI (1956), 300–16.

Bell, John E. "The Family Group Therapist: An Agent of Change," International Journal of Group Psychotherapy, XIV (1964), 72–83.

Belton, Sylvia I., et al. "Group Counseling for College Freshmen by Graduate Students," Washington, D.C., Center for Youth and Community Studies, Howard University, 1965.

Bennis, W. K., et al., *The Planning of Change.* New York, Holt, Rinehart, and Winston, 1961.

Berenson, Bernard G., et al. "The Interpersonal Functioning and Training of College Students," *Journal of Counseling Psychology,* XIII (1966), 441–46.

Berkovitz, Irving H., et al. "Psychosexual Development of Latency-Age Children and Adolescents in Group Therapy in a Residential Setting," *International Journal of Group Psychotherapy,* XVI (1966), 344–56.

Berlin, Irving. "School Child Guidance Services: Retrospect and Prospect," *Psychology in the Schools,* III (1966), 229–36.

Berne, Eric. *Games People Play.* Brattleboro, Vt., The Book Press, 1964.

Bernstein, Saul. *Youth on the Streets—Work With Alienated Youth Groups.* New York, Association Press, 1964.

Berschling, Chester and Juergen Homann. "A Proposal for the Establishment of a Group Psychotherapy Program for Adolescents," *Psychiatric Communications,* VIII (1966), 17–36.

Biermann, G. "Group Therapy in Children and Adolescents with Behavior Disorders and their Parents," *Prax. Kinderpsycol.* (Ger.), XIII (1964), 40.

Bion, W. R. *Experience in Groups.* New York, Basic Books, 1961. (see also Review by Bach, *International Journal of Group Psychotherapy,* XII (1962), 523).

Boenheim, C. "Group Psychotherapy with Adolescents," *International Journal of Group Psychotherapy,* VII (1957), 398–405.

Borgatta, E. F., and R. F. Bales. "Interaction of Individuals in Reconstituted Groups," *Sociometry,* XVI (1953), 302–20.

——— "Task and Accumulation of Experience as Factors in the Interaction of Small Groups," *Sociometry,* XVI (1953), 239–52.

Borgatta, E. F., et al. "On the Dimensions of Group Behavior," *Sociometry,* XIX (1956), 222–40.

——— "The Spectrum of Individual Interaction Characteristics: An Interdimensional Analysis," *Psychol. Rep. Monogr. Suppl.,* IV (1958), 279–391.

Bowen, Murray. "The Family as the Unit of Study and Treatment: I. Family Psychotherapy, Workshop, 1959," *American Journal of Orthopsychiatry,* XXXI (1961), 40–60.

Boy Scouts of America. *Boy Scout Manual: A Handbook for Boy Scouts.* National Council Boy Scouts of America, New Brunswick, N.J., 1959.

Bradford, L. P., et al. *T-Group Theory and Laboratory Method.* New York, Wiley, 1965.

Braverman, Shirley. "The Informal Peer Group as an Adjunct to Treatment of the Adolescent," *Social Casework,* XLVII (1966), 152–57.

Briggs, Dennie L. "Convicted Felons as Social Therapists," *Corrective Psychiatry and Journal of Social Therapy,* IX (1963), 122.

Brodey, W. M. "The Family as the Unit of Study and Treatment: III. Image, Object and Narcissistic Relationships, Workshop, 1959," *American Journal of Orthopsychiatry,* XXXI (1961), 69–73.

Burdon, Arthur P., et al. "Emotionally Disturbed Boys Failing in School: Treatment in an Out-Patient Clinic School," *Southern Medical Journal,* LVII (1964), 829.

Butcher, T., et al. "Scholastic Suicide: An Emerging Problem Area for Community Mental Health," *American Journal of Orthopsychiatry,* XXXV (1965), 346.

Calderwood, Deryck, and Leila den Beste. "Developing Open Communication About Sex with Youth," *Journal of Marriage and the Family,* XXVIII (1966), 524–26.

Caplan, Lloyd M. "Identification, A Complicating Factor in the Inpatient Treatment of Adolescent Girls," *American Journal of Orthopsychiatry,* XXXVI (1966), 720–24.

Carrothers, Marie Lawrence. "Sexual Themes in an Adolescent Girls' Group," *International Journal of Group Psychotherapy,* XIII (1963), 43–51.

Cartwright, Dorwin, and Alvin Zander, eds. *Group Dynamics— Research and Theory.* Evanston, Ill., Row, Peterson, 1953.

Center for Youth and Community Studies. *Training for New Careers.* Washington, D.C., Office of Juvenile Delinquency and Youth Development, HEW, 1965.

Chestnut, W. J. "The Effects of Structured and Unstructured Group Counseling on Male College Students' Underachievement," *Journal of Consulting Psychology,* XII (1965), 388.

Clements, Barton E. "Transitional Adolescents, Anxiety and Group Counseling," *Personnel and Guidance Journal,* XLV (1966), 67–71.

Cohn, I. H. "Intra-Psychic Changes in an Adolescent Girl during Group Psychotherapy," in *Group Psychotherapy Today—Topical Problems of Psychotherapy,* Vol. V, ed. A. L. Kadis and C. Winick. New York, S. Karger, 1965.

Coser, L. A., and B. Rosenberg. *Sociological Theory, A Book of Readings*. New York, Macmillan, 2nd ed., 1964.

Daniels, Ada M. "Training School Nurses to Work with Groups of Adolescents," *Children*, XIII (1966), 210–16.

Daniels, Edward M., et al.. "A Group Approach to Predelinquent Boys, Their Teachers and Parents, in a Junior High School," *International Journal of Group Psychotherapy*, X (1960), 346–52.

Day, G. A. "A Program for Teen-Age Unwed Mothers," *American Journal of Public Health*, LV (1965), 978.

Durkin, Helen E. "Analysis of Character Traits in Group Therapy," *International Journal of Group Psychotherapy*, I (1951), 133–43.

——— *The Group in Depth*. New York, International Universities Press, 1965.

Duffy, J. H., and I. A. Kraft. "Group Therapy of Early Adolescents: An Evaluation of One Year of Group Therapy with a Mixed Group of Early Adolescents," *American Journal of Orthopsychiatry*, XXXV (1965), 372.

Elliott, Delbert S., et al. "Dropout and the Social Milieu of the High School: A Preliminary Analysis," *American Journal of Orthopsychiatry*, XXXVI (1966), 808–17.

Empey, Lamar T. *Pinehills*. Los Angeles, Calif., Youth Development Center, University of Southern California, 1965.

——— *A Social System Approach for Working in Small Groups with Socially Deprived Youth*. Los Angeles, Calif., Youth Studies Center, University of Southern California, 1966.

———, and Jerome Rabow. "The Provo Experiment in Delinquency Rehabilitation," *American Sociology Review*, XVI (1961), 679.

Epstein, Norman. "Delinquent Interactions Between Middle-Class Male Adolescents and their Parents and Implications for Group Psychotherapy," presented at American Group Psychotherapy Conference, Philadelphia, Pa., 1966.

———, and S. R. Slavson. " 'Breakthrough' in Group Treatment of Hardened Delinquent Adolescent Boys," *International Journal of Group Psychotherapy*, XII (1962), 199–210.

Erickson, E. H. *Identity and the Life Cycle*. New York, International Universities Press, 1959.

Evans, John. "Analytic Group Therapy with Delinquents," *Adolescence*, I (1966), 180–96.

Feder, Bud. "Limited Goals in Short-Term Group Psychotherapy with Institutionalized Delinquent Adolescent Boys," *International Journal of Group Psychotherapy,* XII (1962), 503–507.

Federal Bureau of Prisons. "Pre-Release Guidance Center Demonstration Project," in The Fourth Annual Conference on Juvenile Delinquency, Laurel, Md., 1963.

Fenton, Norman. *A Handbook on the Use of Group Counseling in Juvenile and Youth Correctional Institutions.* Sacramento, Calif., Institute for the Study of Crime and Delinquency, 1965.

Festinger, Leon. "Group Attraction and Membership," *Journal of Social Issues,* VII (1951), 152–63.

Field, Lewis W. "An Ego-Programmed Group Treatment Approach with Emotionally Disturbed Boys," *Psychological Reports,* XVIII (1966), 47–50.

Fitzsimmons, Carol J. "Change in Self-Concept of Adolescents in Residential Treatment," *Smith College School of Social Work Abstracts of Theses,* XXXVII (1966), 35–36.

Flint, A. A., Jr., and Beryce W. MacLennan. "Some Dynamic Factors in Marital Group Psychotherapy," *International Journal of Group Psychotherapy,* XII (1962), 355–61.

Foulkes, S. H., and E. J. Anthony. *Group Psychotherapy: The Psychoanalytic Approach.* London, Penguin Books, 1957.

Fraiberg, Selma H. "Studies in Group Symptom Formation," *American Journal of Orthopsychiatry,* XVII (1947), 278.

Franklin, Girard H. "Group Psychotherapy with Delinquent Boys in a Training School Setting," *International Journal of Group Psychotherapy,* IX (1959), 213–18.

French, J. R. P., Jr. "Disruption and Cohesion of Groups," *Journal of Abnormal and Social Psychology,* XXXVI (1941), 391.

Freud, S. *Group Psychology and the Analysis of the Ego* (1921). New York, Leveright, 1951.

Frey, Louise A., and Ralph L. Kolodny. "Group Treatment for the Alienated Child in the School," *International Journal of Group Psychotherapy,* XVI (1966), 321–37.

Fried, Edrita. "Ego Emancipation of Adolescents Through Group Psychotherapy," *International Journal of Group Psychotherapy,* VI (1956), 358–73.

—— "Ego Functions and Techniques of Ego Strengthening," *American Journal of Psychotherapy,* III (1955), 407.

Friedenberg, E. A. *The Vanishing Adolescent.* New York, Dell, 1959.

Friedlander, Kate. "Varieties of Group Therapy Patterns in a

Child Guidance Service," *International Journal of Group Psychotherapy,* III (1953), 59–65.

Fry, Charles L. "Training Children to Communicate to Listeners," *Child Development,* XXXVII (1966), 675–85.

Gabriel, Betty. "Group Therapy for Adolescent Girls," *American Journal of Orthopsychiatry,* XIV (1944), 593.

Gadpaille, Warren J. "Observations on the Sequence of Resistances in Groups of Adolescent Delinquents," *International Journal of Group Psychotherapy,* IX (1959), 275–86.

Gersten, Charles. "An Experimental Evaluation of Group Therapy with Juvenile Delinquents," *International Journal of Group Psychotherapy,* I (1951), 311–18.

———— "Group Therapy with Institutionalized Juvenile Delinquents," *Journal of Genet. Psychology,* LXXX (1952), 35.

Gibbons, I. L. "Day Care: A Mental Health Intervention," *Child Welfare,* XLV (1966), 140–44.

Godenne, G. D. "Outpatient Adolescent Group Psychotherapy I: A Review of the Literature on the Use of Co-Therapists, Psychodrama, and Parent Group Therapy," *American Journal of Psychotherapy,* XVIII (1964), 584.

———— "Outpatient Adolescent Group Psychotherapy: II. Use of Co-Therapists, Psychodrama, and Parent Group Therapy," *American Journal of Psychotherapy,* XIX (1965), 40.

Goffman, Erving. *Asylums.* New York, Doubleday-Anchor, 1961.

Golombek, Harvey. "Group Admission of Adolescents to a Day Program," *Hospital and Community Psychiatry,* XVII (1966), 108–109.

Gottesfeld, H. "Professionals and Delinquents Evaluate Professional Methods with Delinquents," *Social Problems,* XIII (1965), 45.

Grant, J. Douglas, and M. Q. Grant. "A Group Dynamics Approach to the Treatment of Nonconformists in the Navy," *Annals of the American Academy of Political and Social Science,* CCCXXII (1959), 126.

Grant, J. Douglas, et al. *The Offender as a Correctional Manpower Resource: Its Implementation.* Asilomar, Calif., Institute for the Study of Crime and Delinquency, NIMH, 1966.

Grayson, Ellis. "Group Counseling and Group Discussion," in The Fourth Annual Conference on Juvenile Delinquency, Laurel, Md., 1963.

Grunwald, Hanna. "Group Counseling in a Family and Children's

Agency," *International Journal of Group Psychotherapy,* VII (1957), 318–26, and IV (1954), 183–92.

Hall, Edward T. *The Silent Language.* New York, Doubleday, 1959.

Hallowitz, E., and Bernice Stephens. "Group Therapy with Fathers," *Social Casework,* XL (1959), 183.

Hare, A. P. *Handbook of Small Group Research.* New York, The Free Press—Macmillan, 1961.

Hare, A. P., et al. *Small Groups—Studies in Social Interaction.* New York, Knopf, 1955.

Harrington, R. C., et al. "Poor Academic Performance in Bright Adolescent Boys: A Study in Group Psychotherapy," *American Journal of Orthopsychiatry,* XXXV (1965), 345.

Heacock, Don R. "Modifications of Standard Techniques for Out-patient Group Psychotherapy with Delinquent Boys," *American Journal of Orthopsychiatry,* XXXV (1965), 371.

———— "Modifications of the Standard Techniques for Out-Patient Group Psychotherapy with Delinquent Boys," *Journal of the National Medical Association,* LVIII (1966), 41–47.

Head, Wilson A. "Sociodrama and Group Discussion with Institutionalized Delinquent Adolescents," *Insights,* I (1966), 26–39.

Hemphill, J. K., and C. M. Westie. *Group Dimensions: A Manual for their Measurement.* Research Monogr. 87, Bureau of Business Research, Ohio State University, 1956.

Hersko, Marvin. "Group Psychotherapy with Delinquent Adolescent Girls," *American Journal of Orthopsychiatry,* XXXII (1962), 169.

Hill, William, and Ida Hill. *Hill and Hill Interaction Matrix.* Youth Development Center, University of Southern California, 1965.

Hollingshead, H. *Elmtown's Youth: The Impact of Social Classes on Adolescents.* New York, Wiley, 1949.

Homans, G. *The Human Group.* New York, Harcourt, Brace, 1950.

Hyman, H. H. "The Psychology of Status," *Archives of Psychology,* No. 269, 1942.

International Journal of Group Psychotherapy, "Group Dynamics," VI (1956); VII (1957), Nos. 1 & 2; "Three Research Approaches to a Question in the Field of Group Dynamics," XI (1961), No. 3.

Janvier, Carmelite. "Adolescents in Action," *American Journal of Orthopsychiatry,* XIII (1943), 82.

"The Job Corps: A Dialogue," *American Child*, XLVIII (1966), whole issue (no. 1).

Johnsgard, K. W., and G. A. Muench. "Group Therapy with Normal College Students," *Psychotherapy*, II (1965), 114.

Jones, Maxwell. *The Therapeutic Community: A New Treatment Method in Psychiatry*. New York, Basic Books, 1953.

Josselyn, I. W. *The Adolescent and His World*. New York, Family Service Association of America, 1952.

Kaldeck, Rudolph. "Group Psychotherapy with Mentally Defective Adolescents and Adults," *International Journal of Group Psychotherapy*, VIII (1958), 185–92.

Kassoff, Arthur I. "Advantages of Multiple Therapists in a Group of Severely Acting-Out Adolescent Boys," *International Journal of Group Psychotherapy*, VIII (1958), 70–75.

Kimbro, Exall L., et al. "A Multiple Family Group Approach to Some Problems of Adolescence," *International Journal of Group Psychotherapy*, XVI (1966).

King, C. "Activity Group Therapy," in *Group Psychotherapy Today—Topical Problems of Psychotherapy*, Vol. V, eds. A. L. Kadis and C. Winick. New York, S. Karger, 1965.

―――― "Group Therapy with Delinquents In and Out of Institutional Settings," *American Journal of Orthopsychiatry*, XXXV (1965), 259.

Klein, Malcolm W., and Barbara G. Myerhoff, eds. *Juvenile Gangs in Context: Theory, Research, and Action*. University of Southern California Conference Report, 1963.

Koch, Sigmund. *Psychology—Study of a Science*. Vols. II, III, V, VI. New York, McGraw-Hill, 1959.

Konopka, Gisela. *Social Group Work: A Helping Process*. Englewood Cliffs, N. J., Prentice-Hall, 1963.

Kraft, Irvin A. "The Nature of Sociodynamics and Psychodynamics in a Therapy Group of Adolescents," *International Journal of Group Psychotherapy*, X (1960), 313–20.

―――― "Some Special Considerations in Adolescent Group Psychotherapy," *International Journal of Group Psychotherapy*, XI (1961), 196–203.

Lay, T. "Stimulating Communication Among Nonverbal Boys," *Journal of Correctional Psychiatry and Social Therapy*, XI (1965), 261.

Leary, Thomas. *The Interpersonal Diagnosis of Personality.* New York, Ronald, 1957.

Levin, Tom. *A Proposal for a Health Career's Institute.* New York, Albert Einstein, 1967.

Lewin, K. *Field Theory in Social Science.* New York, Harper, 1951.

———— *Resolving Social Conflicts.* New York, Harper, 1948.

Lewis, James C., and Norbert Glasser. "Evolution of a Treatment Approach to Families: Group Family Therapy," *International Journal of Group Psychotherapy,* XV (1965), 505–15.

Lewis, O. *The Children of Sanchez.* New York, Random House, 1961.

Lieberman, Florence. "Transition From Latency to Prepuberty in Girls: An Activity Group Becomes an Interview Group," *International Journal of Group Psychotherapy,* XIV (1964), 455–64.

Lindsey, Gardiner. *Handbook of Social Psychology.* Vol. 1: *Theory and Method.* Chaps. 5–6, 10–14. Cambridge, Mass., Addison-Wells, 1954.

Lippitt, R., and R. K. White. "An Experimental Study of Leadership and Group Life," in *Readings in Social Psychology,* ed. T. M. Newcomb. New York, Holt, 1947.

Lippitt, R., et al. *The Dynamics of Planned Change.* New York, Harcourt, Brace, 1958.

Luzzi, Matthew, and Betty Ann Glasser. "Adolescent Patients Join the Neighborhood Youth Corps," *Hospital and Community Psychiatry,* XVII (1966), 172–74.

McCarthy, James E., and Joseph S. Barbaro. "Re-Directing Teen-Age Gangs," in *Reaching the Unreached.* New York City Youth Board, 1952.

McCorkle, Lloyd W. "Guided Group Interaction in a Correctional Setting," *International Journal of Group Psychotherapy,* IV (1954), 199–203.

McCorkle, Lloyd W., et al. *The Highfields Story.* New York, Holt, 1958.

McCormick, C. G. "Objective Evaluation of the Process and Effects of Analytic Group Psychotherapy with Adolescent Girls," *International Journal of Group Psychotherapy,* III (1953), 181–90.

MacGregor, R., et al. *Multiple Impact Therapy with Families.* New York, McGraw-Hill, 1964.

MacLennan, Beryce W. The Analysis of Group Techniques in the Treatment of Negro Adolescent Girls. Unpublished Ph.D Dissertation, Social and Clinical Psychology in the Faculty of Economics, London University, 1960.

———— *"Children's Groups as Socializing and Rehabilitating Agents."* Washington, D.C., Center for Youth and Community Studies, Howard University, 1965.

———— "Group Approaches to the Problems of Socially Deprived Youth: The Classical Psychotherapeutic Model," *International Journal of Group Psychotherapy,* XVIII (1968).

———— "The Group as a Reinforcer of Reality," presented at American Orthopsychiatric Conference, Washington, D.C., 1967.

———— "The Human Service Aide," *Children,* XIII (1966), 190–94.

———— "The Promise of the Neighborhood Youth Corps," in *The Use of Groups in the Treatment of Adolescent Problems: Selected Readings,* eds. B. W. MacLennan and Viera Morse. Washington, D.C., Howard University Institute for Youth Studies, 1966.

————, and K. Burke. "The Use of Groups in Probation." Washington, D.C., Center for Youth and Community Studies, Howard University, 1964.

———— and Melvin Davis. "Group Counseling at the Receiving Home for Delinquent Youth." Washington, D.C., Howard University Institute for Youth Studies, 1966.

———— and William L. Klein. "Utilization of Groups in Job Training," *International Journal of Group Psychotherapy,* XV (1965), 424–33.

MacLennan, Beryce W., et al. "Training for New Careers," *Community Mental Health Journal,* II (1966), 135–41.

Mann, Richard D. "Dimensions of Individual Performance in Small Groups Under Task and Social-Emotional Conditions," *Journal of Abnormal and Social Psychology,* LXII (1961), 674–82.

Merton, R., et al. *Sociology Today.* (Chaps. on Small Groups and Family) New York, Basic Books, 1959.

Meyer, H. J., et al. *Girls at Vocational High: An Experiment in Social Work Intervention.* New York, Russell Sage Foundation, 1965.

Miller, Walter B. "The Impact of a Community Group Work Program on Delinquent Corner Groups," in *Mental Health of the Poor,* Eds. Frank Riessman, et al. New York, Free Press, 1964.

Mitchell, Lonnie E., et al. "A Mobile Therapeutic Community for Adolescents," CYCS, Howard University, 1965.

Montgomery County (Md.) Board of Education. Work-Oriented Curriculum. 1964 (mimeo).

Moreno, J. L. *Who Shall Survive?* Washington, D. C., Nervous and Mental Disease Publishing Co., 1934.

Munzer, Jean. "Acting Out: Communication or Resistance?" *International Journal of Group Psychotherapy,* XVI (1966), 434–41.

Nash, Eva L., et al. "A Collaborative School—Mental Health Program for Disadvantaged Teenagers," presented at American Orthopsychiatric Assn. Conference, Washington, D. C., 1967.

Newman, R. G., et al. *The School Centered Life Space Interview.* Washington, D. C., Washington School of Psychiatry, 1963.

New York City Youth Board. *Reaching the Unreached.* New York, 1952.

Parsons, T. *The Social System.* New York, The Free Press—Macmillan, 1951.

————, and R. F. Bales. *Family Socialization and Interaction Process.* New York, The Free Press—Macmillan, 1957.

Pearl, Arthur, and Frank Riessman. *New Careers for the Poor.* New York, Free Press, 1965.

Peck, H. B., and Virginia Bellsmith. *Treatment of the Delinquent Adolescent.* New York, Family Service Association of America, 1964.

Perl, William R. "Benefits from Including One Psychopath in a Group of Mildly Delinquent Patients," *International Journal of Group Psychotherapy,* VI (1956), 77–79.

———— "Use of Fantasy for a Breakthrough in Psychotherapy Groups of Hard-to-Reach Delinquent Boys," *International Journal of Group Psychotherapy,* XIII (1963), 27–33.

Perry, Ethel. "The Treatment of Aggressive Juvenile Delinquents in 'Family Group Therapy'," *International Journal of Group Psychotherapy,* V (1955), 131–49.

Persons, Roy W., and Harold B. Pepinsky. "Convergence in Psychotherapy with Delinquent Boys," *Journal of Counseling Psychology,* XIII (1966), 329–34.

Pilnick, Saul, et al. "The Essexfields Concept: A New Approach to the Social Treatment of Juvenile Delinquents," *Journal of Applied Behavioral Science,* II (1966), 109–24.

Powdermaker, Florence B., and J. D. Frank. *Group Psychotherapy: Studies in Methodology of Research and Therapy.* Cambridge, Harvard University Press, 1953.

Rainwater, Lee. "Crucible of Identity: The Negro Lower Class Family," *Daedalus,* XCV (1966), 172–216.

Redl, F. "Group Emotion and Leadership," *Psychiatry,* V (1942), 573–96.

Richmond, Alvin H., and Shirley Schecter. "A Spontaneous Request for Treatment by a Group of Adolescents," *International Journal of Group Psychotherapy,* XIV (1964), 97–106.

Riessman, Frank. *The Culturally Deprived Child.* New York, Harper, 1962.

Robinson, J. "Venture in Group Psychotherapy in the Senior High School," *National Assn. Deans of Women,* XVII (1964), 25.

Rose, Dorian M., et al. "Play Group Therapy with Psychotic Adolescent Girls," *International Journal of Group Psychotherapy,* IV (1954), 303–11.

Ruesch, J., and G. Bateson. *Communication, The Social Matrix of Psychiatry.* New York, Norton, 1951.

Sadock, Benjamin, and Robert E. Gould. "A Preliminary Report on Short-Term Group Psychotherapy on an Acute Adolescent Male Service," *International Journal of Group Psychotherapy,* XIV (1964), 465–73.

Schachter, S. "Deviation, Rejection, and Communication," in *Group Dynamics—Research and Theory,* eds. Dorwin Cartwright and Alvin Zander. Evanston, Ill., Row, Peterson, 1953.

Scheidlinger, Saul. "Three Group Approaches with Socially Deprived Latency-Age Children," *International Journal of Group Psychotherapy,* XV (1965), 434–45.

Schreiber, M., and M. Feeley. "A Guided Group Experience," (Part I of Siblings of the Retarded) *Children,* XII (1965), 221.

Schulman, Irving. "Dynamics and Treatment of Anti-Social Psychopathology in Adolescents," *Nervous Children,* XI (1955), 35.

———— "The Dynamics of Certain Reactions of Delinquents to Group Psychotherapy," *International Journal of Group Psychotherapy,* II (1952), 334–43.

———— "Modifications in Group Psychotherapy with Anti-Social Adolescents," *International Journal of Group Psychotherapy,* VII (1957), 310–17.

Shaw, M. C., and R. Wursten. "Research on Group Procedures in Schools: A Review of the Literature," *Personnel and Guidance Journal,* XLIV (1965), 27.

Sheldon, W. D., and T. Landsman. "An Investigation of Non-Directive Group Therapy with Students in Academic Difficulty," *Journal of Consulting Psychology,* XIV (1950), 210.

Shellow, Robert S., et al. "Group Therapy and the Institutionalized Delinquent," *International Journal of Group Psychotherapy,* VIII (1958), 265–75.

Sherif, M., and H. Cantril. *Psychology of Ego Involvement.* Princeton, N. J., Princeton University Press, 1947.

Siegel, M. "Group Psychotherapy with Gifted Underachieving College Students," *Community Mental Health Journal,* I (1965), 188.

Silver, Albert W. "A Therapeutic Discussion Group in a Detention Home for Adolescents Awaiting Hospital Commitment," *International Journal of Group Psychotherapy,* XIV (1964), 502–503.

Slavson, S. R. *Analytic Group Psychotherapy.* New York, Columbia University Press, 1950.

——— "Patterns of Acting Out of a Transference Neurosis by an Adolescent Boy," *International Journal of Group Psychotherapy,* XII (1962), 211–24.

——— *The Practice of Group Therapy.* New York, International Universities Press, 1947.

——— *Re-Educating the Delinquent.* New York, Free Press, 1965.

——— *A Textbook in Analytic Group Psychotherapy.* New York, International Universities Press, 1964.

Slavson, S. R., et al. "Group Therapy with Adolescent Delinquent Boys," *International Journal of Group Psychotherapy,* X (1960), 174.

Sohn, L. "Group Therapy for Young Delinquents," *British Journal of Delinquency,* III (1952), 20.

Solomon, J. C., and Pearl L. Axelrod. "Group Psychotherapy for Withdrawn Adolescents," *Disturbed Children,* LXVIII (1944), 86.

Spergel, I. "Selecting Groups for Street Work Service," *Social Work,* X (1965), 47.

Spotnitz, H. "Observations on Emotional Currents in Interview Group Therapy with Adolescent Girls," *Journal of Mental and Nervous Disorders,* CVI (1947), 565.

Stanton, R., and M. Schwartz. *The Mental Hospital.* New York, Basic Books, 1965.

Stauffer, Marjorie. "Group Psychotherapy in a Family Agency," *International Journal of Group Psychotherapy,* I (1951), 348–55.

Sternlicht, M. "Establishing an Initial Relationship in Group Psychotherapy with Delinquent Retarded Male Adolescents," *American Journal of Mental Deficiency,* LXIX (1964), 39.

Stock, D., and H. Thelen. *Emotion Dynamics and Group Culture.* Washington, D. C., National Training Laboratories, 1958.

Stranahan, Marion, et al. "Activity Group Therapy with Emotionally Disturbed and Delinquent Adolescents," *International Journal of Group Psychotherapy,* VII (1957), 425–36.

——— "Group Treatment for Emotionally Disturbed and Potentially Delinquent Boys and Girls," *American Journal of Orthopsychiatry,* XXVII (1957), 518–27.

Stubblebone, J., and R. Roadruck. "Treatment Program for Mentally Deficient Adolescents," *Journal of Mental Deficiency,* LX (1956), 552.

Thorpe, J. J., and B. Smith. "Operational Sequence in Group Therapy with Young Offenders," *International Journal of Group Psychotherapy,* II (1952), 24–33.

——— "Phases in Group Development in the Treatment of Drug Addicts," *International Journal of Group Psychotherapy,* III (1953), 66–78.

Tolman, Norman G. "Approaching the Institutionalized Female Delinquent Through Group Therapy," *Federal Probation, XXVIII* (1964), 41.

Vinter, Robert D., and Rosemary C. Sarri. "Malperformance in the Public School: A Group Work Approach," *Social Work,* X (1965), 3.

Walker, W. L., and L. E. Mitchell. "Group Decision-Making in an Apprenticeship Program for Youth," *American Journal of Orthopsychiatry,* XXXV (1965), 378.

Webb, A. P., and J. Eikenberry. "A Group Counselling Approach to the Acting-Out Pre-Adolescent," *Psychology in the Schools,* I (1964), 395.

Wellington, J. "Group Therapy with Pre-Adolescent Girls," *Psychotherapy,* II (1965), 171.

Westman, Jack C. "Group Psychotherapy with Hospitalized Delinquent Adolescents," *International Journal of Group Psychotherapy,* XI (1961), 410–18.

Whitaker, D. S., and M. A. Lieberman. *Psychotherapy Through the Group Process.* New York, Atherton Press, 1964.

Wohl, S. T. "A Project in Group Counselling in a Junior High School," *Personnel and Guidance Journal,* XLII (1964), 611.

Wolff, Kurt W. *The Sociology of Georg Simmel.* Glencoe, Ill., Free Press, 1950.

Wolk, R. L., and R. Ried. "A Study of Group Psychotherapy Results with Youthful Offenders in Detention," *Group Psychotherapy,* XVII (1964), 56.

Wollan, K. I. "Application of Group Therapy Principles to Institutional Treatment of Adolescents," *International Journal of Group Psychotherapy,* I (1951), 356–64.

Yalom, Irvin D. "Compatibility and Cohesiveness in Therapy Groups," *Archives of General Psychiatry,* XV (1966), 267–75.

——— "A Study of Group Therapy Dropouts," *Archives of General Psychiatry,* XIV (1966), 393–414.

Index